ROBERT LOUIS
STEVENSON

His Associations with Australia

Introduced by Robert Darroch

ETT IMPRINT
Exile Bay

Published by ETT Imprint, Exile Bay 2022

First published in a limited edition of 30 copies by George Mackaness 1935
Reprinted by Review Publication 1976, 1982
First electronic edition ETT Imprint 2021

Compiled by Tom Thompson

ISBN 978-1-922473-38-7 (paper)
ISBN 978-1-922384-39-4 (ebook)

Design by Hanna Gotlieb
Cover, photographs and Timeline by Tom Thompson

ROBERT LOUIS STEVENSON

Etched by W. Strong after a photograph by Falk

The Union Club, Bligh Street, Sydney in 1890.

CONTENTS

RLS by Charles Kerry, Sydney 1893.

INTRODUCTION

Robert Louis Stevenson (he pronounced it "Lewis") made four visits to Australia, beginning with his first in 1890. He spent a total of more than five months in Sydney, staying mainly in the exclusive Union Club, of which he was a reciprocal guest (by dint of his membership of The New Club in Edinburgh).

Unlike the other famous literary figures who fetched up in Sydney (Mark Twain, Trollope, DH Lawrence, Conrad, Kipling, Conan Doyle, Charles Darwin, etc.), Stevenson made an effort to mix with local society and meet many prominent cultural and literary figures. "I have tried to lay myself out to be sociable," he told his brother back in Scotland.

An important survey of Stevenson's time in Sydney was written in 1935 by Australian bibliophile George Mackaness, a one-time English master at Fort Street School. He undertook considerable research into Stevenson's time in Sydney and interviewed a number of people who had met the author of *Treasure Island* while he was there.

His monograph *Robert Louis Stevenson: his Associations with Australia* is probably the best account of a literary visitor's time in Australia. It certainly deserves comparison with Lawrence's *Kangaroo,* who borrowed Stevenson's initials for his eponymous character Richard Lovatt Somers.

Indeed, the parallel goes much further. While in Australia, Stevenson dictated to his stepson, who was with him, a novella *The Wrecker* which, like *Kangaroo,* was partly set in Sydney and the coast south of NSW. Even more curiously, the book inspired an episode of the 1950's TV series *Maverick* which involved James Garner following up the plot of Stevenson's novella (and whose credits conceded its link to *The Wrecker*).

While in Sydney, Stevenson visited the famous artists' camp at Balmoral and invited the doyen of Australian painting Julian Ashton to dine with him at the Union Club (which preserves in its library the chair Stevenson favoured when reading or writing at the Club).

Stevenson stayed at other places in Sydney. including the Oxford Hotel opposite St James's Church in King Street – where he put up his visiting mother, wife Fanny and his American-born stepson - and in a mansion in Hunters Hill named after a town in Samoa.

As Mackaness recounts in his sketch, Stevenson's main purpose coming to Sydney was to engage an architect to draw up plans for the house he intended to build in the hills above the Samoan capital, Apia. It was there, in that house, Stevenson died in 1894, aged only 44. He left his own epitaph:

> *Here he lies where he longed to be,*
> *Home is the sailor, home from sea,*
> *And the hunter home from the hills.*

Robert Darroch

ROBERT LOUIS STEVENSON

His Associations with Australia

Australia has been honoured by the visits of curiously few great literary men, even in recent years when communication is so much more speedy than heretofore. Froude, Charles Darwin, "Orion" Horne, Foster Fraser, Jack London, D. H. Lawrence, Conrad, Kipling, John Galsworthy, and John Masefield have all trodden the soil of the Southern Continent, but our most frequent visitor - the one whose association has been closest with Australia, or at any rate with New South Wales - was the distinguished Scot, Robert Louis Stevenson, whose visits I propose to discuss in this paper.

In the year 1890, Stevenson was living at Apia in Samoa, where he had purchased some three hundred acres in the bush, two miles behind and six hundred feet above the level of the town, and on which he proposed to build a cottage for himself and his family. Why did he almost immediately leave Samoa to pay his first visit to Sydney? The answer, as he tells us himself, was not "for the purpose of spying out the land," but first because he was seeking health, and secondly because he wished to consult an architect regarding the plans for his new home to be built at Vailima. It was on February 17 that he reached Sydney on the German steamer Lubeck. Two weeks later he wrote to Mr. Thomas Stevenson, under date March 5, 1890:-

For myself I am in such a whirl of work and society, I can ill spare a moment. My health is excellent and has been here tried by abominable wet weather and (what's waur) dinners and lunches. As this is like to be our metropolis, I hate tried to lay myself out to be sociable with an eye to yourself. Several niceish people have turned up.

Alas for his hopes and fears! He had to take to his bed almost immediately afterwards - he was staying at the Union Club - for he had caught cold and had a serious haemorrhage, the first for eighteen months. The old prostrating series of disorders -cold, fever and haemorrhage - combined to keep him prisoner in his room on a diet of drugs and egg-nog. It is on March 7 that he wrote to his intimate friend Baxter:-

My dear Charles, - I did not send off the enclosed before from laziness, having gone quite sick and being a blooming prisoner here in the Club and indeed in my bedroom.

Coughing, however, could not quench his humour. His spirit alternated between a deep depression and a glad optimism. Optimism won the victory, for the hope was ever present of a return to Scotland, and so,

..............to behold again in dying
Hills of home! and to hear again the call,
Hear about the graves of the martyrs the peewees crying,
And hear no more at all.

Mr. J. A. Stewart declares that he became so cheerful that he yearned to entertain himself with his beloved flageolet, "only the rules of the Union Club forbade performances which might cause a breach of the peace." " Conceive my impatience," he again writes, " to be in my own backwoods, and raise the

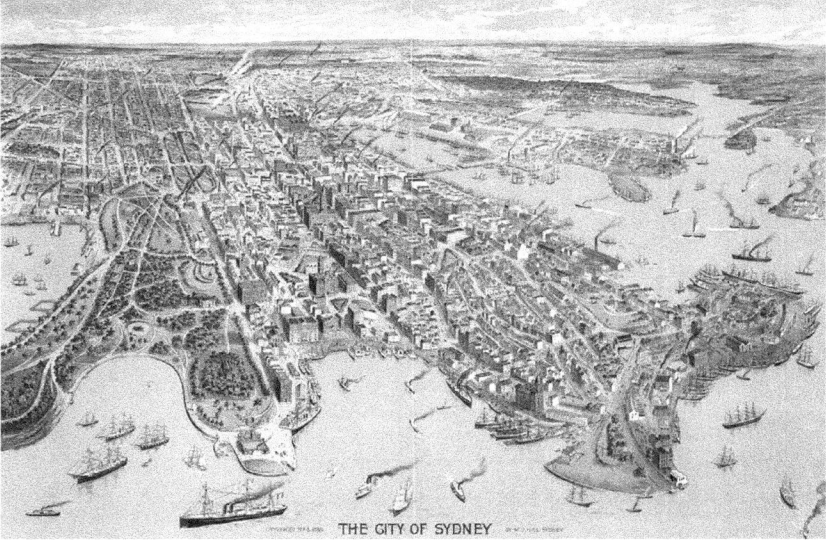

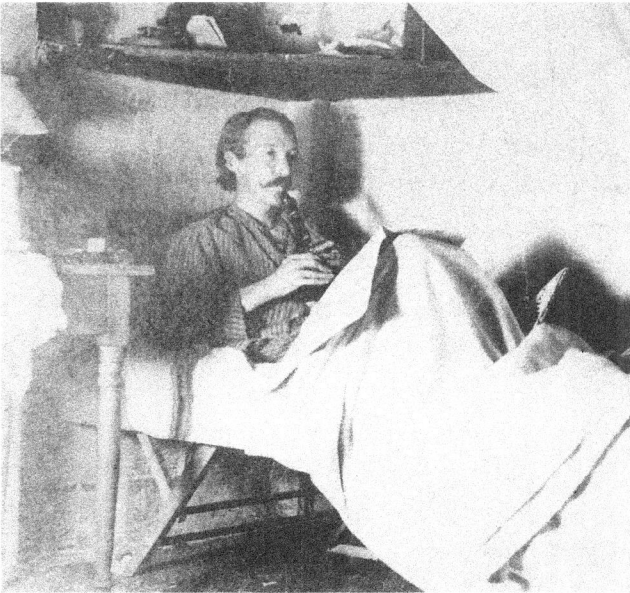

Sydney as RLS saw it. Below: RLS playing the flageolet.

sounds of minstrelsy. What pleasures are to be compared with those of the Unvirtuous Virtuoso?"

Though he himself was in residence at the Union Club, his family was staying in lodgings. Soon after his arrival he was measured for a dress suit and other clothing by Chorley, the tailor - the firm still has the particulars in their books of many items supplied, for they became not only his tailors but his general outfitters - but he made little use of his fine feathers. On this visit he met comparatively few people, the chief being those who called upon him. He did, however, grant interviews to the Press. To one presswoman, Mme. Rose-Soley - a delightful old lady still living, who wrote two articles on R. L. Stevenson in U.S.A., and who herself recently recounted to me the story of her visits to the novelist - he talked almost entirely on Samoan affairs, Malietoa, the German influence, and the prospects of trade with the island.

Towards the end, however, we learn a little about his literary activities. Mme. Rose-Soley asked him whether, during his tour of the south seas, he had visited Treasure Island. Mr Stevenson smiled humorously and said:

Treasure Island is not in the Pacific. In fact, I only wish myself that I knew where it was. When I wrote the book I was careful to give no indication of its whereabouts for fear there might be an undue rush towards it. However it generally supposed to be in the West Indies. But to be serious my next work of fiction will be called The Wrecker, *and will deal with the career of a wreck in the Pacific.*

He outlined the plot, stating that there would be no heroine and no love episodes, and added:-

I am afraid that I have not been altogether successful with my heroines in the past, and intend to amid any mistakes of this kind in the future.

He told the interviewers that, in collaboration with Lloyd

Osbourne, he was also working out a more serious book dealing with Samoa. Then he grew angry at the suggestion that his association with Lloyd Osbourne was based commercially on the fact that Lloyd Osbourne was an American citizen, and therefore that any joint production would necessarily be copyright in U.S.A. He said that he had lost a great deal of money through Americans pirating his books. Even though he sent proofs of a new book to his American publishers a few days before the English publication, that did not prevent his work being exploited by unscrupulous American publishers. "There were at least twenty-five American pirated editions of Kidnapped in circulation." He made a strong plea for a system of international copyright. Discussing his own work, he said:-

In my own practice I try to represent what is conspicuous and representable in the world about me ..... I try to do so on the whole to give pleasure and rouse interest... I believe in looking to the characters and passions, getting over the ground and appealing to the strong, common sentiments directly.

As to the methods of his work, he stated: -

I like to have several hooks in hand at the same time, because l find that the whole secret of sustained intellectual effort lies in turning opportunely from one story to another. Thus, although apparently entirely occupied with the immediate work in hand, one part of the brain is starting up new ideas.

He knew little of Australian writers, but expressed his intention of reading Marcus Clarke's *Natural Life*; "and when I have time, I am going to study your poetry."

How far he succeeded in this one cannot say.

Finally, he spoke at length and with some feeling on certain tendencies in modern fiction, his thesis being summed up in the phrase, " Candour in fiction." Zola he trounced unmercifully. " Zola I consider the victim of sexual insanity." His influence was bad, whereas the plain-spokenness of Fielding and his school never proved offensive to English readers. '' I do not,'' said Stevenson, "approve of the English prudery of the present day... I believe that the people will eventually revert to the plain-speaking habits of their ancestors."

I have just mentioned the writing of *The Wrecker*. Though Stevenson was still seriously ill, there were several days when he was able to stroll about the city with Lloyd Osbourne, his stepson, and to secure a little local colour for this story. If you care to re-read that book, you will find the whole of Chapter XXII., ''The Remittance Man,'' based on Stevenson's Sydney associations, particularly his strolls in the Domain and his trip down the South Coast.

One passage in particular is well worth transcribing:-

The long day and longest night he [Carthew] spent in the Domain; now on a bench, now on the grass under a Norfolk Island pine, the companion of perhaps the lowest class on earth, the larrikins of Sydney. Morning after morning the dawn behind the lighthouse recalled him from slumber; and he would stand and gaze upon the changing east, the fading lenses, the smokeless city, and the many-masted harbour growing slowly clear under his eyes. His bed-fellows (so to call them) were less active; they lay sprawled upon the grass and benches, the dingy men, the frowsy women, prolonging their late repose... Day bought a new society of nurserymaids and children, and fresh-dressed and (I am sorry to say) tight-laced maidens [this was in 1890], and gay people in rich traps; upon the skirts of which Carthew and '' the other black-guards "- his own bitter phrase-skulked, and chewed grass, and looked on... The round of the night began again, the loitering women, the lurking men, the sudden out-burst of screams, the flying feet... Yes, it's a queer place, where the dowagers and the kids walk all day, and at night you can hear people bawling for help as if it was the Forest of Bondy, with the lights of a great town all round, and parties spinning through in cabs from Government House and dinner with my lord!

In the final stage of *The Wrecker* and the *Letters* which he was writing for an American syndicate, he produced sixty thousand words in a month - "elephant's work," he remarked. Yet it made him "sick to think of Scott turning out *Guy Mannering* in three weeks." 'Heavens!' he exclaimed furiously, " "what thews and sinews!" He envied, too, the flexibility of mind which enabled Scott to turn from one subject, one interest, to another, "with a brain that was ever fresh and nimble." Lovers of Scott and Stevenson will find an interesting chapter in Mr. J. A. Steuart 's book, wherein he contrasts these two great Scotsmen.

Just one other sidelight before we leave *The Wrecker* – Stevenson's humorous and satiric comments on English as spoken at the Antipodes (p. 324). He tells of Hemstead, the unemployed shopkeeper's assistant:-

"They 're a dyngerous lot of people about this park. My word! it doesn't do to ply with them," he observed, in that *rycy* Australian English which (as it has received the imprimatur of Mr. Froude) we should all make haste to imitate.

Of the sights of Sydney, Stevenson tells us little. Yet he did gaze upon our General Post Office, and was not at all impressed by it. " An ungainly structure with a tower," is how he describes it. Though he never saw Melbourne, he was even more caustic in his criticism. " "When I think of Melbourne," he once said, " I vomit! ... Its flatness, its streets laid out with a square rule, are certain to have a detrimental effect on those who are doomed to dwell by the yellow waters of the Yarra."

I have been at some pains to interview a number of those who met Stevenson during one or other of his four visits to Sydney. Since many of these, speaking from memories of over forty years ago, have not been able definitely to recall the year to which particular events refer, I have been compelled in some instances, relying upon internal evidence, to associate the incidents chiefly with the last, and longest visit - that of 1893.

Undoubtedly the strongest Stevensonian link with Australia is the publication of his famous *Damien Letter*, written at the Union Club in 1890. Several stories are told regarding how it came to be written. Dr. Robert Scot-Skirving, so it is recorded [1], met Stevenson one day early in March, and asked him what he was doing with himself. "Well," said he, "I propose to devote myself to writing a libel, but it will be a justified and righteous one." It seems that on the previous evening, over the dinner table, reference had been made to Father Damien and the Molokai lepers. Someone asked Stevenson if he had seen a letter written by the Rev. Dr. Hyde, a Presbyterian minister in Honolulu, whom Stevenson had met there. It was addressed to the Rev. H. B. Gage, and was printed in the Sydney Presbyterian. It will be remembered that in May, 1889, Stevenson had himself visited Molokai and spent, by special permission, a week at the leper settlement. Father Damien had died on April 15, so that it must also be kept in mind that Stevenson heard only by report of the man whose memory he was to do so much to vindicate. In the "Hyde" letter the gravest aspersions were cast on the moral character of Damien, the leper priest of Molokai. When Stevenson read the account, he leaped to his feet in furious anger, declaring that he must reply at once - must smash the traducer of a dead man for whom he had conceived an ardent admiration. So the famous defence was written, and stands now almost exactly as it was in the first hastily written draft.

There is a story, repeated by Graham Balfour, to the effect that about the same time Stevenson had heard a report that

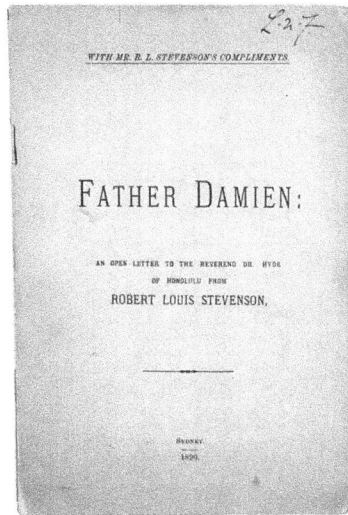

WITH MR. R. L. STEVENSON'S COMPLIMENTS

FATHER DAMIEN:

AN OPEN LETTER TO THE REVEREND DR. HYDE
OF HONOLULU FROM
ROBERT LOUIS STEVENSON.

SYDNEY.
1890.

RLS's chair in the Library at the Union Club, Sydney.
Below: Father Damien, and the rare Sydney edition by RLS.

a proposed memorial to Damien in London had been abandoned on account of this or some similar statement. Let Mr. J.M. Sanders now take up the story.[2]

I was managing Editor of the *Australian Star* Newspaper at the time of the publication in that paper of Robert Louis Stevenson's *Open Letter to Dr. Hyde* in vindication of the life work and personal character of Father Damien. I was personally acquainted with Stevenson. Before the letter was written I had an interview with him, and in the course of conversation he expressed his intention of replying to Dr. Hyde's attack. Stevenson's chief anxiety appeared to be the space he would require and the possibility of editorial amendment and emendment of his expressed thoughts. I satisfied him upon both points. That was on a Thursday. The following afternoon (Friday) he gave me his MS., and the following day (24th March) the "Open Letter", was published for the first time in the *Australian Star*. The letter, which was entitled *IN DEFENCE OF THE DEAD*, took up practically the whole of the front page of the paper, and was accompanied by a portrait of the author an intimate study from life executed by Mr. Lloyd Osbourne, Stevenson's stepson, and completed only a few weeks before the publication of the letter ..... The letter appeared upon the front page of every issue of the Australian Star on the day of its publication, the circulation of the paper covering some 45,000.[3]

According to Mr. Graham Balfour, Stevenson had the courage of his opinions, and realised the risks he was taking, for he stated:-

I knew I was writing a libel : I thought he would bring an action : I made sure I should be ruined; I asked leave of my gallant family, and the sense I was signing away all I possessed kept me up to high water mark, and made me feel every insult heroic.

Stevenson's fears were, however, unjustified. Dr. Hyde

IN DEFENCE OF THE DEAD.

DAMIEN, OF MOLOKAI.

R. L. Stevenson to Dr. Hyde.

A Scathing Criticism.

R. L. STEVENSON.

It is some time now since the death of Father Damien was first made widely known to the world the noble work among the unfortunate lepers of Molokai to which he had

to express the individual, or who perhaps, were only blinded and silenced by generous admiration, such as I partly envy for myself—such as you, if your soul were enlightened, would envy on your bended knees. It is the least defect of such a method of portraiture that it makes the path easy for the devil's advocate, and leaves for the misuse of the slanderer a considerable field of truth. For the truth that is suppressed by friends is the readiest weapon of the enemy. The world, in your despite, may perhaps owe you something if your letter be the means of substituting once for all a credible likeness for a wax abstraction. For, if that world at all remember you on the day that Damien of Molokai shall be named saint, it will in virtue of one work: Your letter to the Rev. H. B. Gage.

You may ask ask on what authority I speak. It was my inclement destiny to become acquainted not with Damien but with Dr. Hyde. When I visited the lazaretto Damien was already in his resting grave. But such information as I have I gathered on the spot in conversation with those who knew him well and long—some, indeed, who revered his memory, but others who had sparred and wrangled with him, who beheld him with no halo; who, perhaps, regarded him with small respect, and through whose unprepared and scarcely partial communications the plain, human features of the man shone on me convincingly.

THESE GAVE ME

what knowledge I possess; and I learnt it on that scene where it could be most completely and sensitively understood. Kalawao, which you have never visited, about which you have never so much as endeavored to inform yourself; for, brief as your letter is, you have found the means to stumble into that confession. "Less than one half the island," you say "is devoted to the leper." Molokai—"Molokai shine," the "gray," lofty and most desolate island—along all its northern side plunges a front of precipice into a sea of unusual profundity. This range of cliff is, from east to west, the true end and frontier of the island. Only in one spot there projects into the ocean, a certain triangular and ragged down, grassy, stony, winding, and rising in the midst into a hill with a dead crater, the whole bearing to the cliff that overhangs it somewhat the same relation as a bracket to a wall. With this hint you will now be able to pick out the leper station on a map. You will be able to judge how much of Molokai is thus cut off between the surf and the precipice, whether less than a half, or less than a quarter, or a fifth, or a tenth, or say a twentieth, and the next time you burst into print you will be in a position to share with us the issue of your calculations.

I imagine you to be one of those persons who talk with cheerfulness of that place which oxen and wain ropes could not drag you to behold. You, who do not even know its situation on the map, probably denounce sensational descriptions, stretching your limbs the while in your pleasant parlor on

I BELIEVE MY SECT—

and that in which my ancestors laboured, which has enjoyed, and partly failed to utilize, an exceptional advantage, in the islands of Hawaii. The first missionaries ignored the letter.

Bibliographically the Father Damien story is interesting. In the Mitchell Library are two copies of what is known as the Sydney edition of the *Open Letter to Dr. Hyde* - in reality the first edition in book form, and one of the "high spots" most sought after by collectors of Stevenson. The story of its publication, as far as I have been able to piece it together from a number of often conflicting accounts, is as follows. After (probably the next day after) the letter appeared in the *Star*, several well-known city men, including the late Hon. John T. Toohey, his brother, the late James M. Toohey, M.L.A., and the late Frank B. Freehill, suggested to Mr. Sanders the publication of the letter in pamphlet form, for the purpose of supplying the mission of which Father Damien was a member, and certain others interested, with copies of the document in a form more compact and convenient than a copy of the newspaper. To this Mr. Sanders agreed, and the friends named above had the job carried out and bore the expense. The work was entrusted, apparently, to a member of the "Cercle Francais," which Stevenson had once or twice visited. The printer was W. M. Maclardy, who conducted the Ben Franklin Printing Works, then located in Market Street. Only twenty-five copies of the book were published, the title page reading:-

With Mr. R. L. Stevenson's Compliments.

FATHER DAMIEN

An Open Letter to the Reverend Dr. Hyde

of Honolulu from

Robert Louis Stevenson

Sydney

1890.

It is a pamphlet of thirty-two pages without covers. Though the author's name is printed at the end, it bears no printer's imprint. Perhaps Maclardy knew the danger surrounding the issue of so libellous a publication. The date of publication is given by Graham Balfour as March 27, 1890.

In *The Australasian* (July 29, 1922) appeared a very interesting letter from Mr. James Grant, then of Leura. He said:-

I well remember Dr. Hyde's letter, which, as stated, appeared in a Sydney newspaper. It sought to belittle the work of Damien among the lepers, and plainly said, ' 'He was not a moral man in his relations with women." At that time (1890) I was employed at the old Ben Franklin Printing Office, the proprietor of which was a member of the Cercle Francais, a coterie of literary and musical men whose meeting place was (the Cosmopolitan Club) in Wynyard Square. R. L. Stevenson had come to Sydney from Samoa. . . . . I do not think his visit made much stir, but the "Cercle" entertained him, and to my employer was entrusted the job of printing the "Apologia." It was only a small job - I think 100 copies, demy 8vo. After completion the parcel went through my hands, and according to office custom, the packer had slipped one copy beneath the string of the parcel to indicate its contents. I took it out, and thought it read like the work of a writer straining for effect, and was somewhat theatrical. The parcel was duly sent out, while the specimen I had looked at went into the w.p.b. A few days later I came across a number of spare copies left as samples, and known as "overs" being in excess of the number ordered. These finally found their way to a large pack which was a receptacle for the office rubbish. A few years afterwards I read that at Sotheby's sale in London a copy of the pamphlet bearing my old employer's imprint[4] had brought at auction £50. I had thrown away £600.

Within the last few years, copies of this edition of the Damien Letter have been sold at prices ranging between £15 and £100, according to their associational value.

The history of the later printings is equally interesting. First, the story circulated by a correspondent in the *Sydney Morning Herald* that an edition of one hundred copies was either printed and published, or at any rate published and offered for sale, by Turner and Henderson, seems to have no foundation. A search of their records reveals no trace of any such edition; neither is it mentioned in any of the Stevenson bibliographies.

In Mr. Arthur Johnston's volume, *Robert Louis Stevenson in the Pacific*, there is a chapter entitled "The Hurling of the Damien Letter." He tells how the booklet was first republished at Honolulu from an advance copy sent to the editor of the *Elele*, a journal at that time published both in the English and the Hawaiian tongues. Edition after edition was struck off to supply the local demand, and thousands of copies were printed as a broadsheet to meet the demand of outlying islands and elsewhere. I recently had the pleasure of examining one of these broad-sheets in the collection of Mr. J. A. Ferguson of Sydney. A proposal was next made that the letter should be translated and published in the native edition of the *Elele*. After some deliberation, however, the four directors decided against the suggestion.

In the same years (1890) appeared in Edinburgh the second privately printed edition, thirty copies only, a royal 8vo. printed on Japan paper and bound in vellum hoards, each copy being accompanied by a portrait of Father Damien loosely inserted.[5] Of this edition I noted that a copy in 1928 brought thirty-five dollars at auction in America.

Copies of the letter were also sent to certain English papers, including *The Times*, and to *The Scot's Observer*, in which it appeared on May 3 and 10. What is usually known at the first published edition was issued by Chatto and Windus in brown paper wrappers in 1890 at one shilling.

James Milne, in *The Memoirs of a Bookman* (p. 46), writing of Sir George Grey, said:-

What would one not have given to listen to a long talk he and Robert Louis Stevenson once had on a ship in Sydney Harbour. He [Grey) drew a vivid picture of that meeting for me, and as a token of it, gave me a copy of the famous Father Damien Pamphlet, presented to him at the time by R.L.S. Alas! that treasure, with corrections in blue pencil by the author, took wings, but another relic of Sir George Grey, his pioneer book on the mythology of the Maoris, is as well preserved as when he wrote his name in it.

Now that forty odd years have elapsed, criticism generally inclines to castigate Stevenson for the violence of his attack on Dr. Hyde. Even he himself, when coolness and reflection induced a saner, better-balanced judgment, regretted the violence of its tone. He confessed it was "barbarously harsh," and that he might have defended Damien equally well without inflicting pain on others.

Of the friendships made on this first and renewed on his subsequent visits I shall speak later. On April 10 he telegraphed to Mr. Baxter: "Return Islands four months. Home September." He was now seriously ill, and pining for the sea and Vailima. After great difficulty, Mrs. Stevenson secured passages on a small trading steamer of six hundred tons, the *Janet Nicholl*, where he met and immortalised the famous trio to whom *An Island Night's Entertainment* was afterwards dedicated-Mr. Henderson, one of the partners; Ben Hird, the super-cargo; and Jack Buckland, the living original of Tommy Haddon in *The Wrecker*.

After calling for a day at Auckland, they put in at Apia, enabling Stevenson to inspect his new property. They then proceeded to the Gilbert and Marshall Islands, visiting in

RLS (top right) and Fanny (seated left) with the crew of the
Janet Nicholl. *Below: RLS (right) and Fanny on Butaritari.*

all some thirty-five islands. On the return journey the *Janet Nicholl* called at New Caledonia, where Stevenson stayed for a few days by himself, allowing his wife and stepson to return direct to Sydney. By the end of August, however, he was back in Sydney with his family, "trying to adjust himself and his affairs to altered conditions."

Again his health was very bad, compelling him to spend a deal of his time in bed at the Union Club, where he toiled at his South Sea Letters, "at my old trade - bedridden. " During his second sojourn with us, he was much worried about the improvements he intended to make at his home, Vailima. He consulted a Sydney architect, and got him to draw a plan. "If I haven't anything else to thank Sydney for," he told his friend Moors on his return to Apia, "I've got this plan. It suits me exactly; it's simply wonderful. You'll be delighted with it." Unfortunately the plan could not be adhered to, as it entailed an expenditure of several thousands of pounds. In the *Life of Mrs. Stevenson* there is a story told by Mrs. N. V. Sanchez, which, though inaccurate in details, is worth recording. She states that on their return to Sydney, in island attire, and encumbered with island curios and impedimenta, they applied for rooms at Sydney's leading hotel. On being refused, they made application at the Old Oxford Hotel where they were courteously received. When, next morning, the newspapers devoted much space to the arrival of the world-famous writer, and three times a day a bag of letters had to be sent from the first hotel round to the "Oxford," the proprietor of the former begged Stevenson to return, and as a non-paying guest, but the novelist refused point blank, and on later occasions always had his family accommodated at the "Oxford." On this visit Stevenson met and became friendly with Bernhard R. Wise, a well-known constitutional lawyer. Some years later Wise recorded his recollections of Stevenson.

Many will remember evenings in the old French Club, or at the Australian and Athenaeum Clubs, which became mornings before Stevenson's gaiety and brilliant talk allowed the company to leave. He was grave and gay by turns, turning from shrewd but kindly criticism of life or books to wild extravaganza in the style of his own New Arabian Nights. France was very dear to him, and he talked much of French artistic life, its fun, its contentment, its humorous half-pathetic miseries. . . . . Stevenson had a touch of Rabelais's large-hearted gaiety, without the Rabelaisian coarseness.

Sydney had again proved unkind, Stevenson and Mrs. Stevenson (Lloyd Osbourne had left for England) sailed on the *Lubeck* in October for Samoa and Vailima, where he said he hoped to be more than "a pallid weevil in a biscuit." To the trip home I found an interesting reference in the *Autobiography* of the Rev. James Chalmers (p. 350). From Malua, Samoa, Chalmers wrote on September 26, 1890 :-

We had rather a rough passage here (from Sydney). . . . . Louis Stevenson and his wife were on board, and we enjoyed the trip well. They have bought 400 acres of land behind Apia and are going to squat... We had a rather rough passage, but the smoking room was well patronised and we spent many happy hours in it with our new friends ..... My dear wife often said "How gentle and lovable he is, just one to nurse."

The friendship with Chalmers ripened, for in December Stevenson himself wrote:-

Christmas I go to Auckland to visit Tamate, the New Guinea Missionary, A man I love.

Sydney next saw Stevenson in January, 1891, when, leaving his wife in sole charge at Vailima, he went to Sydney to meet his mother, who was to arrive there from Scotland on her way to Samoa. From the letters of Mrs. Margaret Stevenson, Ste-

OBJECTS OF PITY;

OR,

SELF AND COMPANY.

BY

A GENTLEMAN OF QUALITY.

Imprinted at Amsterdam.

The Oxford Hotel, King Street, Sydney in 1890.
The Sydney edition of Objects of Pity, *1892.*

venson's mother, we gather the story of that visit. She says that she found her "dear boy" looking brown and well at the Oxford Hotel. On Sunday afternoon they walked through the Domain, and, after listening to the various orators, came to the conclusion that "a walk through the Domain on a Sunday afternoon is at least not monotonous."

As originally planned, Mrs. Stevenson proposed to travel to New Zealand after seeing her son. As usual, Stevenson " fell sharply sick in Sydney," and, as his condition became rapidly worse, he was brought straight from his bed on board the *Lubeck*, with his mother in constant attendance. This was on February 19, 1891. Mr. C. H. Bertie quotes the letter (to Sidney Colvin) in which Stevenson sums up this particular visit:-

It is vastly annoying that I cannot go down to Sydney without an attack and heaven knows my life was anodyne; at the Club with Wise; worked all morning, - a terrible dead pull, a month only produced the imperfect embryos of two chapters; lunched in the boarding-house; played on my pipe; went out and did some of my messages; dined at a French restaurant, and returned to play draughts, whist or Van John with my family. This makes a cheery life after Samoa, but it isn't what you call burning the candle at both ends, is it?

Though Stevenson was not in Sydney in 1892, that year has for the Stevensonian bibliomaniac the utmost attraction. In a bookseller's catalogue I came upon the following item:-

An Object of Pity, or the Man Haggard, A Romance by Many Competant Hands. (Parchment wrappers.) Imprinted at Amsterdam (n.d.).

This item was called by Mr. Gosse "the most unattainable of Stevenson's productions." Indeed it is so rare that there is not a copy even in the Mitchell Library. The whole story does not concern us here. Suffice it is to say that this little book of some sixty-eight pages was the work of Stevenson, Mrs.

Stevenson, Mrs. Strong, and a little circle of Samoan friends, including the Countess of Jersey, wife of the Governor of New South Wales, and her brother. Mr. James H. Mulligan, U.S.A. Consul-General for Samoa; Mr. A. W. MacKay, of the Friendly Islands and Samoa; and the Rev. W. E. Clarke, of the London Missionary Society, were also interested. "The Man Haggard" was Mr. Bazett Michael Haggard, a brother of the late Sir Rider Haggard. R. L. Stevenson's own contributions are the "Dedication" (by Tusitala) and Chapter IV., "Late, Ever Late." The Sydney association is explained by Lady Jersey herself in her autobiography:-

An Object of Pity *was written by my brother and myself in collaboration with the Stevensons… As for the booklet, with general agreement of the authors I had it privately printed in Sydney - Mr. Gosse says he thinks there were only 35 copies - the copies being distributed amongst us. Some years after Stevenson's death, in November, 1898, Mr. Blaikie (of Constables) asked permission to print 25 presentation copies in the same form (8vo. buckram) as the Edinburgh edition, to which Mrs. Stevenson consented.*

There were three facsimiles in colour of sketches by Isobel Strong, and Lady Jersey herself wrote an introductory note, in which occurs the following:-

It is needless to say that no thought of even such perpetuity as private circulation may confer, was originally in the minds of the writers, but when they had shared in the reading, they became unwilling to totally lose this record of many happy hours, and agreed to a few copies being privately printed at Sydney, with the mysterious statement on the title-page, "Imprinted at Amsterdam.". Had we, who were leaving the Enchanted Island, realised how soon our days there would have receded into a marvellous dream, from which the magician who endowed all things around him with life and romance would have passed away for ever, we should have clung even more closely to every memory which it was possible to retain.

The only copies I ever saw catalogued were of the Sydney edition at £33 (Edwards), and one of the second edition at £35. Though there is no edition of either in the Mitchell, that Library possesses a copy of Mr. Bazett Haggard 's Reply:-

OBJECTS OF PITY,

or

SELF AND COMPANY

By

A Gentleman of Quality

Imprinted at Amsterdam.

(n.d.)

Mr. Haggard was H.B.M.'s Land Commissioner at Samoa.

In every way Stevenson's fourth visit to Sydney in 1893 was the most important. He arrived on February 28, and at once gave interviews to the Press. Mr. J. Tighe Ryan, editor of the *Catholic Press*, who became very friendly with Stevenson, asserts:-

It cannot be said that the appearance of this world-famed author caused at any time a flutter of excitement in Sydney. In 1893 I remember quite well the S.M. Herald *interviewed him upon his arrival on the prospects of trade with Samoa. I am not sure that they even spoke of him as a man of letters, or that the interviewer did not mistake him for an island merchant. The reporters stated that he was in good health and he assured them that the reports of his death which had reached Sydney, were, as Mark Twain said in a similar position, "greatly exaggerated."*

On this visit he lived in a number of places - at the Oxford Hotel in King Street; at the Union Club; in rooms in Macquarie Street; for a week as the guest of Dr. Andrew Garran, then editor of the *Sydney Morning Herald*; and in what Dr. Scot-Skirving calls "rather forbidding apartments in St. Mary's Terrace,

Domain," and adds:-

There I spent an evening. He, his beautiful old mother, Graham Balfour, later his biographer, and I think, his step-daughter, Mrs. Strong, were there. It was a most jovial evening, and we agreed that only "the braid Scots tongue should be spoken." How we clattered in the vernacular at which R. L. Stevenson was a pastmaster, as all who know his "Underwoods" will believe! What fun it was!

Dr. Scot-Skirving had been one of the Fleming Jenkin Circle in Great Stuart Street, Edinburgh, had associated with Stevenson there, and joined with him in private theatricals.

 Mr Scot-Skirving writes: -

Many years later, after I had settled in Sydney, Stevenson came there more than once. I rang him up at his hotel, for in Sydney we had telephones even then, and his voice replied - I remembered it at once. He had a marked but agreeable Lothian accent. He said, "Are you the man who acted at the Jenkins' theatricals?" I modestly said that I had been call-boy! He then came to my house, and I spent various evenings with him. He was very full of writing an account of the navigational knowledge of the South Sea Islanders as explanatory of the populating islands so widely separated from each other. He never carried out this piece of work. I talked much with him on this subject and on sea-things. He had a good landman's knowledge of ships, but not a technically correct one, as some errors in his sea-stories show.

Reminiscences of Stevenson's last visit to Sydney are numerous. As his health was much better he went about more, met hosts of people, chiefly the literary and artistic folk, and was lionised generally. He paid a visit to the University, visited the Royal Exchange and signed the visitors' book. He had his photograph taken several times by Kerry, which he described as "splendid." In a letter dated May 29, 1893, to the sculptor St. Gaudens, who had made a medallion of him in New York, Stevenson wrote:-

Fanny, RLS, Belle and Margaret Stevenson by Freeman.
Portrait of RLS by Barnett of Falk Studios, Sydney.

The other day in Sydney I think you might be interested to hear, I was sculpt a second time by a man named Leyselle as well as I can remember and read. I mustn't criticise at present, and he had very little time to do it. It was thought by my family to be an excellent likeness of Mark Twain.

Stevenson was invited to Government House, but refused to attend "unless," as he told Rupert Carrington, "he could wear his favourite white suit" - generally worn with a red cummerbund.

To pressmen he willingly gave interviews. To the representative of the *Australian Star* (March 4, 1893) he talked for two columns on Samoan affairs, and then told how he was writing three short stories of the South Seas to be called *Island Nights' Entertainment*. He discussed the appropriateness of the titles of his stories, regretting that in one of his books, *Virginibus Puerisque*, he had made a serious blunder in his choice, for many modest young women, when asking a bookseller for the book, used to refrain from mentioning it by name, preferring to say "Mr. R. L. Stevenson's latest book." He said, too, that he had on hand "one story of Scotland in 1813, another of Scotland and England in 1814, another of France and Scotland in 1749, a South Sea story of the present day, and a short narrative of the Californian Coasts ten years ago. That's all, I think."

Stevenson made the acquaintance of Archibald of the *Bulletin*, who took him across to the famous artists' camp or colony of the day at Balmoral. There he met Julian Ashton, Streeton, Tom Roberts, A. J. Daplyn, B. E. Minns, and many others, including Percy Spence, who did a pencil sketch of him, now in the National Portrait Gallery, London.[7] Tighe Ryan, writing in *The Antipodean* in 1893, tells how Stevenson "chummed up with the cook at the camp, 'Old Ben,' a stranded, weather-beaten sea-dog full of reminiscences from all quarters of the

Fanny Stevenson by Freeman of Sydney, 1893.
RLS by Percy Spence, Sydney 1893.

world." Ben is now recognised in one of the novelist's books, and is (or was) the possessor of a presentation signed copy of *Treasure Island*. David Souter, the artist, told me recently that "Old Ben", is immortalised as the original of Julian Ashton's painting, "The Prospector." To *The Antipodean* Stevenson also contributed a poem, "To My Old Familiars" (Vol. II., p. 14), the decorations being by Percy Spence. With Julian Ashton, "the grand old man of the art world of Sydney," he became very friendly, frequently visiting his house. A few months ago Mr. Ashton himself was good enough to chat with me over his Stevensonian associations. He told me how, on one occasion, visiting Stevenson at the Union Club, he found him in bed, but dressed. Mr. Ashton continued:-

Throwing me a little blue paper-covered volume, he said: "That fellow has genius. Have you ever seen anything of him? By God, imagine that name for a novelist, Rudyard Kipling. A man with a name like that couldn't help writing." The little book was one of the early Indian Railway Library editions.

Pointing to a waste paper basket filled with scraps of MS., he said to Mr. Ashton:-

See that! Man, the stuff in that basket the publishers would give me golden guineas for, but it doesn't help the story.

B. R. Wise asked Mr. Ashton and Sir Julian Salamons to dine with Stevenson at the Union Club. Salamons was intimately acquainted with French literature, and soon began on it, but found he had met his match in Stevenson, who stalked up and down the room flooding them with his intimate talk about his favourite hobby. When Stevenson's mother came out to Sydney, Mr. Ashton met her. She possessed a most delightful Scotch accent, and, discussing her son, once said to him: "Aw! Mr. Ashton, he canna draw a woman." To Julian Ashton, Stevenson presented a copy of

Graham Balfour   Mrs. Osbourne

Hon. B. R. Wise

Robert Louis Stevenson   Mrs. Thomas Stevenson

RLS and family at the home of Bernhard Wise, Sydney.
Below: Bernhard Wise (left) and Sydney lawyer, Julian Salamons.

the Sydney edition of the Father Damien Pamphlet. Like Mr. Milne's copy, it, too, has taken wings.

Sir Robert Garran, at whose father's house, "Strathmore, " Glebe Point, Stevenson stayed for a week, has also been good enough to write down for me his memories of that brief period of association with the writer. It was at "Strathmore" that one or two of the chapters of *The Wrecker* were written. Sir Robert says:-

Stevenson used to say that there was material for a dozen buccaneering stories to be picked up in the hotels at Circular Quay. He seemed to have a gift for picking up piratical sailor men on the Quay, and getting the best out of them...

He was a delightful conversationalist in a small company, but he hated anything like an "At Home," or large gathering. This opinion he affirmed to more than one of his friends. As he told Tighe Ryan, "he stood in dread of conventional society, of the first class passengers of life, and the man in the tall hat and the neat necktie. That kind of life," he said, "breeds cads." He succeeded in getting a very bad cold while with us, and Mrs. Stevenson nursed him assiduously. He would lie in bed, propped up with pillows alternately writing and playing on his flageolet, or "penny whistle" as he called it. He was very disgusted with the Sydney weather that year, and called the colony "New South Pole."

I remember very little of his conversation - it was largely of his books and travels. The abiding impression is of a picturesque figure in a velvet jacket - almost unbelievably thin and pale - with extraordinary grace and charm of manner, and full of fun and cheerfulness, even when ill. And his conversation was "Stevensonian" all the time, full of wit and humour. One thing I remember his saying ,was that he could find no amusement in a pun. A pun, at the best, might be ingenious, and therefore admirable, but he could see no reason why people should be expected to laugh or even to smile at it... I also remember

his describing his mode of collaboration with Lloyd Osbourne...
Their practice was first of all to talk over a chapter together, planning
it out, just roughly, then in detail, without putting pen to paper.
Then Osbourne would write out a draft, which Stevenson would
re-write or revise.

Madame Rose-Soley, that delightful French lady now very
advanced in years, who in 1890 interviewed Stevenson, has
supplied an anecdote or two. She asserts that he offered his
Damien Pamphlet to the *Sydney Morning Herald*, whose editor
refused to publish it; that Mrs. R. L. Stevenson could be both
fascinating and detestable; and that both his wife and Mrs.
Strong continually pushed him to write.

Tighe Ryan, however, gives us perhaps the most intimate
picture. He tells of Stevenson:

Sitting in his pyjamas on the side of his bed, cigarette in mouth,
his feet bare, on a side table a glass of sherry with which he occasion-
ally moistened his lips, - the room in great disorder - his discourse
fanciful, brilliant and playful, unlike anything one has ever heard
before, the large eyes alight with humour, a rare sweet-ness and
power in the smile - that was the first sight and the first impression
I had of Stevenson.

Of the visits made by Stevenson in Sydney, two or three
stand out conspicuously. He was the guest of the General
Assembly of the Presbyterian Church at luncheon on March
14, 1893, the Moderator presiding. His speech was a brilliant
one, and was recorded verbatim in *The Presbyterian*. Merely to
read it is a delight. Stevenson said:-

I thought when I came here today that perhaps a text would be
suitable. (Laughter.) The first text that occurred to me was this, "Is
Saul also among the prophets?" Then, upon second thoughts, which
I believe we have the authority of our forefathers for saying are better
thoughts, it occurred to me that I had a very good right to appear

here. In the first place I am a Scotsman - (Cheers) - but I will not dwell upon that thrilling story. (Cheers and laughter.) In the second place I am an old, and I hope I may be allowed to say, a very good Presbyterian, the proof of which is that I have sat out a sermon of an hour and thirty minutes. (Laughter.) It was delivered in the parish church of Wick, and by a remarkable coincidence the parish church is still standing in support of my statement. (Laughter.) It was delivered by the Minister of Keiss, one of the most delightful-looking old gentlemen I ever saw in my life. In the third place, I am a grandson of the Manse, and a great-grandson of the Manse. (Applause.) My grandfather was minister of a parish close to Edinburgh. He was not famous for being anything but a nice old gentleman. (Laughter.) As for my great-grandfather, he has been placed in an historical position by Robert Burns. He was Dr. Smith of Galston,-"Smith opens out his cauld harangues." (Applause.)

Stevenson told the Assembly one excellent story which will bear repetition:-

My uncle went down to a graveyard in some strange parish, and there found a worthy-looking man engaged in digging a grave. "Have you much affliction in the parish lately?" said my uncle. The man stopped, put down his spade, and, looking up into his face, rubbed his hands, with the reply, "Affliction! Why I have nae buried three since Lammas!" (Laughter and cheers.)

Stevenson was also set down to address the Women's Missionary Association at an afternoon tea held at Quong Tart's Rooms. Owing to her son's indisposition, Mrs. Stevenson attended and read a paper on "Missions in the South Seas," which had been prepared by her distinguished son.[9]

Of Stevenson's friendship with Professors Anderson Stuart and Liversidge; with James Chalmers of the Civil Service Co-operative Society, and later of Farmer and Company; and with Dr. Fairfax Ross; of his mid-day luncheon at the Cosmopolitan Club, Kowalski presiding, (recalling which F. M. Bladen, late Public Librarian, said, "It was the treat of a lifetime to hear that man speak. I never saw a man who looked so ill. It was a scholarly speech - scholarly and inimitable."); of his visits to Chorley the tailor, and Abbey the bootmaker, space will not allow me to speak in any detail.

Stevenson's holiday - the last but one he was ever to take - was at an end. He left by the *Mariposa*, on which, as one newspaper said, "Mr. and Mrs. Stevenson had to divide the honour of being a distinguished traveller with Griffo and several other boxing celebrities." In a letter to Sir Sidney Colvin, he describes the trip as:-

An amusing but tragic holiday.[10] *Take it all in all, it was huge fun; even Fanny had some lively sport at the beginning.*

All the links binding Stevenson with Australia were, however, not yet forged. A deal of correspondence has taken place in the newspapers regarding the famous Nerli Portraits, one of which was painted in Sydney, another in New Zealand, the third in Vailima. I do not propose to discuss their order of priority or their respective merits.

The Sydney portrait, which has Stevenson's signature on the back, passed into the possession of Angus and Robertson, booksellers, thence to Professor Anderson Stuart, thence to Mr. Fred. Malcolm, and finally to Mrs. Hill, an American collector. This portrait is noteworthy because it is accompanied by a little notebook in which, to lessen the tediousness of sitting, Stevenson wrote some doggerel verses, which I reproduce from a photograph of the original MS.:-

Did ever mortal man hear tell of sae singular a ferlie,
As the coming to Apia here of the painter, Mr. Nerli?
He came and O! for a hunner pound, of a' he was the perli.
He took a thraw to paint mysel', he painted late and early;

0, wow! the many a yawn I've yawned in the beard of Mr. Nerli!

Whiles I would sleep an' whiles would wake, and whiles was mair than surly,

I wondered sair, as I sat there, forninst the eyes of Nerli

'Or will he paint me the way I want, as bonnie as a girlie,

Or will he paint me as an ugly tyke, and be damned to Mr. Nerli?

But still and on and whichever it is, he is a canty Kerlie;

The Lord proteck the back and neck of honest Mr. Nerlie.

Vailima,

Robert Louis Stevenson.

   Samoa. Sept. 1892.

In the Alexander Turnbull Library, Wellington, New Zealand, is an interesting manuscript presented by Mr. W. H. Triggs, a New Zealand journalist. Though the association with Stevenson is Australasian, rather than Australian, the story will serve well to round off this narrative. In his covering letter to Mr. Johannes Andersen, Librarian of the Alexander Turnbull Library, under date April 22, 1931, Mr. Triggs wrote:-

... The story of the way in which it came into my possession supplies yet another instance of Stevenson's proverbial kindness of heart, and the patience and consideration he showed to young writers. In 1893, when I was a young journalist on the staff of the Christchurch Press, I was introduced to Stevenson in Auckland, and he gave me an interesting interview. A few months afterwards, when on a tour of the South Sea Islands, I called at Apia, hoping to see the author in his island home. To my sore disappointment, I found he had gone on a visit to Honolulu. However, I got enough material on the spot, as I thought, to furnish an article on R. L. Stevenson for an English magazine to which I was an occasional contributor. I thought it due to R.L.S., especially after his kindness in the Auckland interview, to let him see the article before publication, and did so with a request that he would strike out any inaccuracies, or any details which he

thought should not be published. By the return mail my draft came back, with these twelve closely written pages of "Annotations" and supplementary information, dictated by Stevenson to his amanuensis, Mrs. Strong, and signed by him. . . .

The original article was published in *Cassell's Magazine* in 1894, shortly before Stevenson's death. It was not, however, till the issue of the *American Bookman*, dated April, 1931, that Stevenson's own annotations and additions were printed in full with (in parentheses) the substance of the passages in the original manuscript which drew forth Stevenson's comments. In the *Bookman* article, readers will find a number of interesting Australian references.

Search of the files of the Christchurch (N.Z.) Press has also discovered the text of Mr. Triggs's first interview with Stevenson. It appeared in the issue of April 24, 1893. There the curious investigator will find Stevenson's considered opinion of the right sort of books to read, and of the best methods to be pursued in the cultivation of a good literary style. Though far too long to quote, it is all well worth examination.

Here let us leave him. His memory, however, still lingers in the minds of many Australians, particularly of the older bookmen, booksellers, and members of the literary and artistic circles of the romantic 'nineties - a vision of the white suit or the black velvet jacket of the famous Scot, whose later years were so closely associated with this land of ours.

SYDNEY LETTERS
AND POEMS

A Modern Novelist

Sydney Morning Herald, Friday 14 February 1890

'I suppose,' said our representative, 'that you will utilise your experience in the South Seas in your next work of fiction. By-the-by, did you visit Treasure Island?'

Mr. Stevenson smiled humourously. 'Treasure Island,' he said, 'is not in the Pacific. In fact, I only wish myself that I knew where it was. When I wrote the book I was careful to give no idication as to its whereabouts, for fear that there might be an undue rush towards it. However, it is generally supposed to be in the West Indies. But to be serious. My next work of fiction will be called '*The Wrecker*' and will deal with the career of a wreck in the Pacific.'

'Can a wreck have a career?'

'Certainly, this one has. The scene is laid on the South Pacific Coast, where the vessel is lost, and the wreck is subsequently sold at auction at San Francisco [...] Eventually, of course, they discover the reason for the great value placed on her.'

'How?'

'Well, that's just where it is', said Mr. Stevenson. 'Wild horses wouldn't drag any more out of me at present.

Letter to Henry James

Union Club, Sydney, February 19, 1890.

Here – in this excellent civilised, antipodal club smoking-room, I have just read the first part of your *Solution*. Dear Henry James, it is an exquisite art; do not be troubled by the shadows of your French competitors: not one, not de Maupassant, could have done a thing more clean and fine; dry in touch, but the atmosphere (as in a fine summer sunset) rich with colour and with perfume. I shall say no more; this note is *De Solutione*; except that I – that we – are all your sincere friends and hope to shake you by the hand in June.

Robert Louis Stevenson
signed, sealed and
delivered as his act
and deed
and very thought of very thought,
this nineteenth of February in the year of our
Lord one thousand eight hundred ninety
and nothing.

Letter to his Mother

Union Club, Sydney, March 5, 1890.

My dear Mother,

I understand the family keeps you somewhat informed. For myself I am in such a whirl of work and society, I can ill spare a moment. My health is excellent and has been here tried by abominable wet weather, and (what's waur) dinners and lunches. As this is like to be our metropolis, I have tried to lay myself out to be sociable with an eye to yoursel'. Several niceish people have turned up: Fanny has an evening, but she is about at the end of the virtuous effort, and shrinks from the approach of any fellow creature.

Have you seen Hyde's (Dr. not Mr.) letter about Damien? That has been one of my concerns; I have an answer in the press; and have just written a difficult letter to Damon trying to prepare him for what (I fear) must be to him extremely painful. The answer is to come out as a pamphlet; of which I make of course a present to the publisher. I am not a cannibal, I would not eat the flesh of Dr. Hyde, – and it is conceivable it will make a noise in Honolulu. I have struck as hard as I knew how; nor do I think my answer can fail to do away (in the minds of all who see it) with the effect of Hyde's incredible and really villainous production. What a mercy I wasn't this man's *guest* in the *Morning Star*! I think it would have broke my heart.

Time for me to go! More anon. With love,
R.L.S.

Letter to Charles Baxter

Union Club, Sydney [7 March 1890]
My dear Charles,

I did not send off the enclosed before from laziness; having gone quite sick, and being a blooming prisoner here in the club and indeed in my bedroom. I was in receipt of your letters and your ornamental photo, and was delighted to see how well you looked, and how reasonably well I stood. Again consider the problem in the enclosures. I *believe* – but have yet to consider Samoan prices – that a thousand pounds or at the outside 1250 should erect my house in its first and imperfect state. I am sure I shall never come back home except to die; I may do it, but shall always think of the move as suicidal, unless a great change comes over me, of which as yet I see no symptom.

This visit to Sydney has smashed me handsomely; and yet I

made myself a prisoner here in the club upon my first arrival. This is not encouraging for further ventures; Sydney winter – or I might almost say Sydney spring, for I came when the worst was over – is so small an affair, comparable to our June depression at home in Scotland. I deed not say, my dear Charles, that all you have done for Bob and Henley exactly pleases me. You have nothing to do with either: you acted according to my instructions in making both the loans, whereof no more, an you love me. I must tell you that the Strongs have been behaving excellently. Joe still lives, but in a great and unceasing danger; Belle has been a kind nurse to him; both have lived all this while on their allowance, and not made one penny of debt. I cannot tell you how encouraging this is, and how it reconciles me with life. The pipe is right again; it was the springs that had rusted, and ought to have been oiled. Its voice is now that of an angel; but Lord! here in the club I dare not wake it! Conceive my impatience to be in my own backwoods and raise the sound of minstrelsy. What pleasures are to be compared with those of the Unvirtuous Virtuoso.

Yours ever affctly,

The Unvirtuous Virtuoso,

Robert Louis Stevenson

Letter to Charles Baxter

Private and confidential

Sydney, 12 March [1890]

My dear Charles,

Enclosed please find a libel: you perceive I am quite frank with my legal adviser; and I will also add it is *conceivable* an action might be brought, and in that event *probable* I should be ruined. If you had been through my experience, you would understand how little I care; for upon this topic my zeal is complete and, probably enough, without discretion.

I put myself in your hands, for Henley's sake, not mine. My case is beyond help. This leaves tomorrow the 13th; two weeks later, day for day, it will be followed by presentation copies, which, for all purposes of action, is publication quite enough, is it not? Thus you will have no power to save me, and can, with a light conscience, follow my desires. That is to say:

1st. If you think Henley should try the gamble, you will let him have it.

2nd. If you think Henley shouldn't, you will kindly see whether the *Times*, *Scotsman*, or other leading paper will touch it.

3rd. If none of them will, see if Chatto will issue it as a pamphlet.

N.B. *Of course in no case will I receive any emolument.* Or, if, in your good judgement, you see any other reputable means of publication, I set you free to adopt it.

On the probabilities of action, a barrister here whom I consulted, one of the leaders, (pic) said, "Have you used any epithets – any epithets, you know? Coarse expressions? No? Not called him 'Hell-Hound'? nor 'Atheist'? No? O then, there's nothing in it?" Which is funny, but unhappily not true. What's more to the purpose, his collegues in Honolulu, whom I know, would probably – I think certainly – dissuade him with eagerness. But then there is the Boston Board of Missions – they may be a low lot, I don't know them from Adam – and the trouble may come from there.

I own I cannot see what they would gain, unless revenge. But then sectarian animosity does not reckon, and there is no question, I may find myself nipped between conflicting churches. You must weigh this in considering for Henley. I don't want to give him a serpent for a fish – no offence to eels. On the other hand, you, better than I, can judge if the thing would be apt to help him. It seems to me rather a spirited piece; but of course I am the last to know, and all of us here, knowing Dr. Hyde personally as we do, are perhaps apt to consider it more pungent than it can appear to the outsider. He is a large, dark, smooth, grave, personable man; carries his blue ribbon like a decoration; and looks as though you might have encountered him in Queen Street, arm in arm with Dr. Phin.

Much love,

Robert Louis Stevenson

Letter to Charles Baxter

[Sydney, 20 March 1890]

My dear Doer,

You will receive along with this a document in which you are trustee. It seems elaborate, and dodgy; I trust it is also, as it looks to the layman, perfectly efficacious.

I will inclose here Moors's last letter in which you will see how things go upon Vailima – Stevensonia, as he calls it – and what you may look for in the way of drafts. I think you will agree it is a very kindly letter.

The man himself is a curious being, not of the best character; has been in the labour trade as supercargo; has been partner with Grossmühl, the most infamous trader in these waters, the man who is accused of paying natives with whist counters; has settled down at last in Apia, where everyone owes his money on mortgage, where his business is both large and growing, and where he took a great though secret part in the late war. I was forced to be his guest, rather against my will, for his looks, his round blue eyes etc. went against me, and the repulsion was mutual. However we both got over it, and grew to like each other; and it's my belief he won't cheat me. He is highly intelligent; tells a story well and from a veracious understanding: of all the scores of witnesses I examined about the war, H.J.M. was the only one whom documents invariably corroborated, and also (although the most open enemy of the Germans at the time) appeared to suffer from no bias in the retrospect. He is married to a Samoan, whom he treats kindly, and his oldest girl is in the States at school. I draw you this portrait because the man is necessarily a feature in my business life and has the marring of many of my affairs. You may wonder I should become at all intimate with a man of a past so doubtful, but in the South Seas, any exclusiveness becomes impossible; they are worth mention. The character of my solicitor for instance is extraordinary; and it was perhaps chiefly as a choice of evils that I left my power of attorney with H.J.M. At the same time, he is a man of so strong an understanding, and is so well-to-do, that personally I am not the least alarmed.

Letter to Francis Marion Crawford

Sydney [c. 8 April 1890]
Dear Sir,

I sail in some forty hours back among the islands, which are now more homelike in my eyes than the world to which I once belonged; I have a thousand calls upon my time; I do not know you, it is likely we shall never meet, and I think it not improbable that my literature may ne abominable in your eyes. For all that I sacrifice some of my last moments to send you my salutations and thanks. Years ago I read *Mr. Isaacs*; I did not like it – I suppose I was a fool; and read no more of you, till the other day, when I fell a pray to *Greifenstein*; nd I am now surrounded by your works, and in the middle of *With the Immortals*.

It is reviving to me to know I have a contemporary of your strength; though I suppose you are younger, as I hope you will soar higher and farther than

Your admirer,

Robert Louis Stevenson

P.S. – I trust you will not think I expect an answer; it is my weakness to rush in with encumbering gratitude when I am pleased; but the act suffices. And indeed I cannot now be said to possess such a thing as an address; the ship in which I leave sails with sealed orders, and I myself am ignorant whither I am bound or where I may bring up.

Some of your books – poor waifs! – are to make the same blindfold launch; they will be read in a better climate and in lovelier places than their author dreams of, Italy not being forgotten.

No pure translations in music? A symphony rendered on the piano; an air from the Queen of Night played on the piccolo. And you forget there are *foreign tongues* even in music: Chinese music, of which you speak very lightly, but have you ever heard it? Even my Polynesian music in which I delight, but most Europeans declare to have no sense or loveliness whatever. I think there is nothing so parochial as music, where all [*one word illegible*] with its little patrimony of twelve sounds, chosen, heaven knows how or why, out of the millions possible. But it is just the narrowness of its patrimony that enables it to be so great.

Cablegram to Charles Baxter

Sydney, 10 April 1890
Return Islands four months. Home September.

Letter to Charles Baxter

[Sydney, 10 April 1890]

My dear Charles,

I have been quite knocked over; go back islands four months, pick up again; sail today, I don't know where.

Sealed orders, but I know some of the islands from slips: Suwaruu, Christmass, Penrhynn, Apemama, and Tapinuea: what else? – O Niue: *all these I have no right to mention!* They are surpreised, so keep 'em secret.

And I daresay to you they are all Greek and Hebrew. Persons with friends in the islands should purchase Findlay's *Pacific Directories*: they're the best of reading anyway, and may almost count as fiction.

We are leaving today, April 10th; gone 4 months; we should be back here August 10th. I'll expect a long letter, and a state of accomps, care of Towns. Good-bye, just now. I must not write more: still weak and groggy.

Yours ever aft,

R.L.S.

Only Lloyd, Fanny, and I go. We leave the Strongs here under custody of a bank (where the wild teller grows). Joe still alive, but pretty weedy.

Letter to Henry James

Union Club, Sydney [19 August 1890]

My dear Henry James,

Kipling is too clever to live. The *Bête Humaine* I had already perused in Noumea, listening the while to the strains of the convict band. He is a Beast; but not human, and, to be frank, not very interesting. 'Nervous maladies: the homicidal ward,' would be the better name: O, this game gets very tedious.

Your two long and kind letters have helped to entertain the old familiar sickbed. So has a book called *The Bondman*, by Hall Caine; I wish you would look at it. I am not half-way through yet. Read the book, and communicate your views. Hall Caine, by the way, appears to take Hugo's view of History and Chronology. (*Later*; the book doesn't keep up; it gets very wild.)

I must tell you plainly – I *can't* tell Colvin – I do not think I shall come to England more than once, and then it'll be to die. Health I enjoy in the tropics; even here, which they call sub- or semi-tropical, I come only to catch cold. I have not been out since my arrival; live here in a nice bedroom by the fireside, and read books and letters from Henry James, and send out to get his *Tragic Muse*, only to be told they can't be had as yet in Sydney, and have altogether a placid time. But I can't go out! The thermometer was nearly down to 50° the other day – no temperature for me, Mr. James: how should I do in England? I fear not at all. Am I very sorry? [...] I am sorry about [...] seven or eight people in England, and [...] one or two in the States. And outside of that, I simply prefer Samoa. These are the words of honesty and soberness. (I am fasting from all but sin, coughing, *The Bondman*, a couple of eggs and a cup of tea.) I was never fond of towns, houses, society, or (it seems) civilisation. Nor yet it seems was I ever very fond of (what is technically called) God's green earth. The sea, islands, the islanders, the island life and climate, make and keep me truly happier.

These last two years I have been much at sea, and I have *never wearied*; sometimes I have indeed grown impatient for some destination; more often I was sorry that the voyage drew so early to an end; and never once did I lose my fidelity to blue water and a ship. It is plain, then, that for me my exile to the place of schooners and islands can be in no sense regarded as a calamity.

Good-bye just now: I must take a turn at my proofs.

N.B. – Even my wife has weakened about the sea. She wearied, the last time we were ashore, to get afloat

again. – Yours ever,
R.L.S.

Letter to Marcel Schwob

Union Club, Sydney, August 19th 1890

My dear Mr. Schwob,

Mais, alors, vous avez tous les bonheurs, vous! More about Villon; it seems incredible: when it is put in order, pray send it me.

You wish to translate the *Black Arrow*: dear sir, you are hereby authorised; but I warn you, I do not like the work. Ah, if you, who know so well both tongues, and have taste and instruction – if you would but take a fancy to translate a book of mine that I myself admired – for we sometimes admire our own – or I do – with what satisfaction would the authority be granted! But these things are too much to expect. *Vous ne détestez pas alors mes bonnes femmes? moi, je les déteste.* I have never pleased myself with any women of mine save two character parts, one of only a few lines – the Countess of Rosen, and Madame Desprez in the *Treasure of Franchard*.

I had indeed one moment of pride about my poor *Black Arrow*: Dickon Crookback I did, and I do, think is a spirited and possible figure. Shakespeare's – O, if we can call that cocoon Shakespeare! – Shakespeare's is spirited – one likes to see the untaught athlete butting against the adamantine ramparts of human nature, head down, breach up; it reminds us how trivial we are today, and what safety resides in our triviality. For spirited it may be, but O, sure not possible! I love Dumas and I love Shakespeare: you will not mistake me when I say that the Richard of the one reminds me of the Porthos of the other; and if by any sacrifice of my own literary baggage I could clear the *Vicomte de Bragelonne* of Porthos, *Jekyll* might go, and the *Master*, and the *Black Arrow*, you may be sure, and I should think my life not lost for mankind if half a dozen more of my volumes must be thrown in.

The tone of your pleasant letters makes me egotistical; you make me take myself too gravely. Comprehend how I have lived much of my time in France, and loved your country, and many of its people, and all the time was learning that which your country has to teach – breathing in rather that atmosphere of art which can only there be breathed; and all the time knew – and raged to know – that I might write with the pen of angels or of heroes, and no Frenchman be the least the wiser! And now steps in M. Marcel Schwob, writes me the most kind encouragement, and reads and understands, and is kind enough to like my work.

I am just now overloaded with work. I have two huge novels on hand – *The Wrecker* and the *Pearl Fisher*, in collaboration with my stepson: the latter, the *Pearl Fisher*, I think highly of, for a black, ugly, trampling, violent story, full of strange scenes and striking characters. And then I am about waist-deep in my big book on the South Seas: *the* big book on the South Seas it ought to be, and shall. And besides, I have some verses in the press, which, however, I hesitate to publish. For I am no judge of my own verse; self-deception is there so facile. All this and the cares of an impending settlement in Samoa keep me very busy, and a cold (as usual) keeps me in bed.

Alas, I shall not have the pleasure to see you yet awhile, if ever. You must be content to take me as a wandering voice, and in the form of occasional letters from recondite islands: and address me, if you will be good enough to write, to Apia, Samoa. My stepson, Mr. Osbourne, goes home meanwhile to arrange some affairs; it is not unlikely he may go to Paris to arrange about the illustrations to my *South Seas*; in which case

I shall ask him to call upon you, and give you some word of our outlandish destinies. You will find him intelligent, I think; and I am sure, if (*par hasard*) you should take any interest in the islands, he will have much to tell you. – Herewith I conclude, and am your obliged and interested correspondent,

Robert Louis Stevenson

P.S. – The story you refer to has got lost in the post.

Letter to Andrew Lang

Union Club, Sydney [late August 1890]

My dear Lang,

I observed with a great deal of surprise and interest that a controversy in which you have been taking sides at home, in yellow London, hinges in part at least on the Gilbert Islanders and their customs in burial. Nearly six months of my life has been passed in the group: I have revisited it but the other day; and I make haste to tell you what I know. The upright stones – I enclose you a photograph of one on Apemama – are certainly connected with religion; I do not think they are adored. They stand usually on the windward shore of the islands, that is to say, apart from habitation (on *enclosed islands*, where the people live on the sea side, I do not know how it is, never having lived on one). I gathered from Tembinoka, Rex Apemamae, that the pillars were supposed to fortify the island from invasion: spiritual martellos. I think he indicated they were connected with the cult of Tenti – pronounce almost as chintz in English, the *t* being explosive; but you must take this with a grain of salt, for I know no word of Gilbert Island; and the King's English, although creditable, is rather vigorous than exact. Now, here follows the point of interest to you: such pillars, or standing stones, have no connection with graves. The most elaborate grave that I have ever seen in the group – to

55

ROBERT LOUIS STEVENSON.
FROM THE MEDALLION BY A. ST. GAUDENS

*The household at Vailima - Mrs Margaret Stevenson, Lloyd
Osbourne, RLS and Fanny (left to right in central verandah).
Below: Sidney Colvin (left) and the RLS Medallion by St. Gaudens.*

be certain – is in the form of a raised border of gravel, usually strewn with broken glass. One, of which I cannot be sure that it was a grave, for I was told by one that it was, and by another that it was not – consisted of a mound about breast high in an excavated taro swamp, on the top of which was a child's house, or rather *maniapa* – that is to say, shed, or open house, such as is used in the group for social or political gatherings – so small that only a child could creep under its eaves. I have heard of another great tomb on Apemama, which I did not see; but here again, by all accounts, no sign of a standing stone. My report would be – no connection between standing stones and sepulture. I shall, however, send on the terms of the problem to a highly intelligent resident trader, who knows more than perhaps any one living, white or native, of the Gilbert group; and you shall have the result. In Samoa, whither I return for good, I shall myself make inquiries; up to now, I have neither seen nor heard of any standing stones in that group.

– Yours,

R.L. Stevenson

This letter is in acknowledgment of proofs received from Scribner's of a proposed volume of verse to contain, besides "Ticonderoga: A Legend of the West Highlands" and the two ballads "The Feast of Famine: Marquesan Manners" and "The Song of Rahero: A Legend of Tahiti", a number of the other miscellaneous verses which he had written in the course of his travels.

Letter to Edward L. Burlingame

Union Club, Sydney [Late August 1890]
My dear Burlingame,
Ballads.

The deuce is in this volume (*proofs just received*). It has cost me more botheration and dubiety than any other I ever took in hand. On one thing my mind is made up: the verses at the end have no business there, and throw them down. Many of them are bad, many of the rest want nine years' keeping, and the remainder are not relevant – throw them down; some I never want to hear of more, others will grow in time towards decent items in a second *Underwoods* – and in the meanwhile, down with them! At the same time, I have a sneaking idea the ballads are not altogether without merit – I don't know if they're poetry, but they're good narrative, or I'm deceived.

(You've never said one word about them, from which I astutely gather you are dead set against: 'he was a diplomatic man' – extract from epitaph of E.L.B. – 'and remained on good terms with Minor Poets.')

You will have to judge: one of the Gladstonian trinity of paths must be chosen. (1st) Either publish the five ballads, such as they are, in a volume called *Ballads*; in which case pray send sheets at once to Chatto and Windus. Or (2nd) write and tell me you think the book too small, and I'll try and get into the mood to do some more. Or (3rd) write and tell me the whole thing is a blooming illusion; in which case draw off some twenty copies for my private entertainment, and charge me with the expense of the whole [...] dream

In the matter of rhyme no man can judge himself; I am at the world's end, have no one to consult, and my publisher holds his tongue. I call it unfair and almost unmanly. I do indeed begin to be filled with animosity; Lord, wait till you see the continuation of *The Wrecker*, when I introduce some New York publishers. [...] It's a good scene; the quantities you drink and the really hideous language you are represented as employing may perhaps cause you one tithe of the pain you have inflicted by your silence on, sir, The Poetaster,

R.L.S.

Lloyd is off home; my wife and I dwell sundered: she in lodgings, preparing for the move; I here in the club, and at my old trade – bedridden. Naturally, the visit home is given up; we only wait our opportunity to get to Samoa, where, please, address me.

Have I yet asked you to despatch the books and papers left in your care to me at Apia, Samoa? I wish you would, *quam primum.*   R.L.S.

Poem on Odysseus to Andrew Lang

[Sydney, late August 1890]
1.
Awdawcious Odyshes,
Your conduc' is vicious,
Your tale is suspicious
 An' queer.
Ye ancient sea-roamer,
Ye dour auld beach-comber,
Frae Haggard to Homer
 Ye veer.
2.
Sic veerin' and steerin'!
What port are ye neerin'
As frae Egypt to Erin
 Ye gang?
Ye ancient auld blackguard,
Just see whaur ye're staggered
From Homer to Haggard
 And Lang!

3.

In stunt and in strife
To gang seeking a wife –
At your time o' life
 It was wrang.
An' see! Fresh afflictions
Into Haggard's descriptions An'
the plagues o' the Egyptians
 Ye sprang!
4.

The folk ye're now in wi'
Are ill to begin wi'
Or to risk a hale skin wi'
 In breeks –
They're blacker and better –
(Just ask your begetter)
And far frae bein' better
 Than Greeks.
5.

Ther's your *Meriamun*:
She'll mebbe can gammon That
auld-furrand salmon
 Yoursel';
An' *Moses* and *Aaron*
Will gie ye your fairin'
Wi' fire an' het airn
 In Hell.

I refuse to continue longer. I had an excellent half-verse there, but couldn't get the necessary pendant, and anyway there's no end to such truck.

Yours,

R.L.S.

Letter to Sidney Colvin

Union Club, Sydney [August 1890]

We had a very interesting voyage for some part; it would have been delightful to the end – had my health held out.

That it did not, I attribute to savage hard work in a wild cabin heated like the Babylonian furnace, four plies of blotting-paper under my wet hand and the drops trailing from my brow. For God's sake don't start in to blame Fanny: often enough she besought me not to go on: but I did my work while I was a bedridden worm in England, and please God I shall do my work until I burst.

I do not know any other virtue that I possess; and indeed there are few others I prize alongside of it. Only, one other I have: I love my friends, and I don't like to hear the most beloved of all casting doubt on that affection.

Did you not get the verses I sent you from Apemama?

I guess they were not A.1. verses, but they expressed something you surely could not doubt. But perhaps all my letters have miscarried? A sorrow on correspondence! If this miscarry too? See here: if by any chance this should come to your hand, […] understand once and for all that since my dear wild noble father died no head on earth is more precious to my thoughts than yours.

But all this talk is useless. Know this, I love you, and since I am speaking plainly for once, I bind it upon you as a sacred duty, […] should you be dangerously ill, I must be summoned. I will never forgive you […] if I am not. So long as there is no danger, I do well, do I not? – to consider conditions necessary to my work and health. I have a charge of souls; I keep many eating and drinking; my continued life has a value of its own; and I cannot but feel it. But I have to see you again. That is sure. And – how strangely we are made! – I see no harm in my dying like a burst pig upon some outlandish island, but if you died, without due notice and a chance for me to see you, I should count it a disloyalty...

Letter to Adelaide Boodle

Union Club, Sydney, 1st September 1890

My dear Miss Boodle,

I find you have been behaving very ill: *been* very ill, in fact. I find this hard to forgive; probably should not forgive it at all if Robin Lewison (*RLS alter-ego*) had not been sick himself and a wretched sick-room prisoner in this club for near a month. Well, the best and bravest sometimes fail. But who is Miss Green? Don't know her [...]! I knew a lady of an exceedingly generous and perfervid nature – worthy to be suspected of Scotch blood for the perfervidness – equipped with a couple – perhaps a brace sounds better English – of perfervid eyes – with a certain graceful gaucherie of manner, almost like a child's, and that is at once the highest point of gaucherie and grace – a friend everybody I ever saw was delighted to see come and sorry to see go. Yes, I knew that lady, and can see her now. But who was Miss Green? There is something amiss here. Either the Robin Lewisons have been very shabbily treated, [...] or – and this is the serious part of the affair – somebody unknown to me has been entrusted with the key of the Skerryvore garret. This may go as far as the Old Bailey, ma'am.

But why should I gird at you or anybody, when the truth is we are the most miserable sinners in the world? For we are not coming home, I dare not. Even coming to Sydney has made me quite ill, and back I go to Samoa, whither please address Apia, Samoa – (and remember it is Sámó-a, a spondee to begin with, or Sahmóa, if you prefer that writing) – back I and my wife go to Samoa to live on our landed estate with four black labour boys in a kind of a sort of house, which Lloyd will describe to you. For he has gone to England: receive him like a favour and a piece of cake; he is our greeting to friends.

I paused here to put in the date on the first page. I am precious nearly through my fortieth year, thinks I to myself. Must be nearly as old as Miss Green, thinks I. O, come! I exclaimed, not as bad as that! Some lees of youth about the old remnant yet. […]

My amiable Miss Green, I beg you to give me news of your health, and if it may be good news. And when you shall have seen Lloyd, to tell me how his reports of the South Seas and our new circumstances strike such an awfully old person as yourself, and to tell me if you ever received a letter I sent you from Hawaii. I remember thinking – or remember remembering rather – it was (for me) quite a long respectable communication. Also, you might tell me if you got my war-whoop and scalping-knife assault on le *nommé Hyde*.[…]

I ought not to forget to say your tale fetched me (Miss Green) by its really vile probability. If we had met that man in Honolulu he would have done it, and Miss Green would have done it. Only, alas! there is no completed novel lying in the garret: would there were! It should be out to-morrow with the name to it, and relieve a kind of tightness in the money market much deplored in our immediate circle. To be sure (now I come to think of it) there are some seven chapters of *The Great North Road*; three, I think, of *Robin Run the Hedge*, given up when some nefarious person pre-empted the name; and either there – or somewhere else – likely New York – one chapter of *David Balfour*, and five or six of the *Memoirs of Henry Shovel*. That's all. But Lloyd and I have one-half of *The Wrecker* in type, and a good part of *The Pearl Fisher* (O, a great and grisly tale that!) in MS. And I have a projected, entirely planned love-story – everybody will think it dreadfully improper, I'm afraid – called *Cannonmills*. And I've a vague, rosy haze before me – a love-story too, but not improper – called *The Rising Sun*. (It's the name of the wayside inn where the story, or much of the story, runs; but it's a kind of a pun: it means the stirring up of a boy by falling in love, and how he rises in the estimation of a girl who despised him, though she liked him, and had befriended him; I really scarce see beyond their childhood yet, but I want to go beyond, and make each out-top the other by successions: it should be pretty and true if I could do it.) Also I have my big book, *The South Seas*, always with me, and a sair handfu' – if I may be allowed to speak Scotch to Miss Green – a sair handfu' it is likely to be. All this literary gossip I bestow upon you *entre confrères*, Miss Green, which is little more than fair, Miss Green.

Allow me to remark that it is now half-past twelve o'clock of the living night; I should certainly be ashamed of myself, and you also; for this is no time of the night for Miss Green to be colloguing with a comparatively young gentleman of forty […]. So with all the kindest wishes to yourself, and all at Lostock, and all friends in Hants, or over the borders in Dorset, I bring my folly to an end. Please believe, even when I am silent, in my real affection; I need not say the same for Fanny, more obdurately silent, not less affectionate than I. – Your friend,

Robert – Robin Lewison

(Nearly had it wrong – force of habit.)

Letter to Elizabeth Fairchild

Union Club, Sydney [c. 1 September 1890]
My dear Mrs. Fairchild,
I began a letter to you on board the *Janet Nicoll* on my last

cruise, wrote, I believe, two sheets, and ruthlessly destroyed the flippant trash.

Your last has given me great pleasure and some pain, for it increased the consciousness of my neglect. Now, this must go to you, whatever it is like.

It is always harshness that one regrets. […] I regret also my letter to Dr. Hyde

Yes, I do; I think it was barbarously harsh; if I did it now, I would defend Damien no less well, and give less pain to those who are alive. These promptings of good-humour are not all sound; the three times three, cheer boys, cheer, and general amiability business rests on a sneaking love of popularity, the most insidious enemy of virtue. On the whole, it was virtuous […] to defend Damien; but it was harsh to strike so hard at Dr. Hyde. When I wrote the letter, I believed he would bring an action, in which case I knew I could be beggared […]. And as yet there has come no action; the injured Doctor has contented himself up to now with the (truly innocuous) vengeance of calling me a 'Bohemian Crank,' and I have deeply wounded one of his colleagues whom I esteemed and liked.

Well, such is life. You are quite right; our civilisation is a hollow fraud, all the fun of life is lost by it; all it gains is that a larger number of persons can continue to be contemporaneously unhappy on the surface of the globe. O, unhappy! – there is a big word and a false – continue to be not nearly by about twenty per cent – so happy as they might be: that would be nearer the mark.

When – observe that word, which I will write again and larger – WHEN you come to see us in Samoa, you will see for yourself a healthy and happy people.

Yes, I do; I think it was barbarously harsh; if I did it now, I would defend Damien no less well, and give less pain to those who are alive. These promptings of good-humour are not all sound; the three times three, cheer boys, cheer, and general amiability business rests on a sneaking love of popularity, the most insidious enemy of virtue. On the whole, it was virtuous […] to defend Damien; but it was harsh to strike so hard at Dr. Hyde. When I wrote the letter, I believed he would bring an action, in which case I knew I could be beggared […]. And as yet there has come no action; the injured Doctor has contented himself up to now with the (truly innocuous) vengeance of calling me a 'Bohemian Crank,' and I have deeply wounded one of his colleagues whom I esteemed and liked.

Well, such is life. You are quite right; our civilisation is a hollow fraud, all the fun of life is lost by it; all it gains is that a larger number of persons can continue to be contemporaneously unhappy on the surface of the globe. O, unhappy! – there is a big word and a false – continue to be not nearly by about twenty per cent – so happy as they might be: that would be nearer the mark.

When – observe that word, which I will write again and larger – WHEN you come to see us in Samoa, you will see for yourself a healthy and happy people.

You see, you are one of the very few of our friends rich enough to come and see us; and when my house is built, and the road is made, and we have enough fruit planted and poultry and pigs raised, it is undeniable that you must come – must is the word; that is the way in which I speak to ladies. You and Fairchild, anyway – perhaps my friend Blair – (J Blair Fairchild) we'll arrange details in good time. It will be the salvation of your souls, and make you willing to die.

Let me tell you this: In '74 or 5 there came to stay with my father and mother a certain Mr. Seed, a prime minister or something of New Zealand. He spotted what my complaint was; told me that I had no business to stay in Europe; that I should find all I cared for, and all that was good for me, in the Navigator Islands; sat up till four in the morning persuading me, demolishing my scruples.

And I resisted: I refused to go so far from my father and mother. O, it was virtuous, and O, wasn't it silly! But my father, who was always my dearest, got to his grave without that pang; and now in 1890, I (or what is left of me) go at last to the Navigator Islands. God go with us! It is but a Pisgah sight when all is said; I go there only to grow old and die; but when you come, you will see it is a fair place for the purpose. Flaubert has not turned up; I hope he will soon; I knew of him only through Maxime Descamps.

– With kindest messages to yourself and all of yours, I remain Robert Louis Stevenson

Letter to Andrew Chatto

Union Club, Sydney [September 1890]

Dear Mr. Chatto,

The letter to Dr Hyde is yours, or any man's, I will never touch a penny of remuneration.

I do no stick at murder; I draw the line at cannibalism; I could not eat a penny roll that piece of bludgeoning had gained for me.

I believe you will soon receive sheets of a thin book of ballads from Scribners. Pray put it in the hand of Clarke, Edinburgh; see that the American spellings are removed, see that "O!" is always "O!" and never "Oh!", and bring it out, if you please, on the same terms as *Underwoods*.

With good wishes – (I daresay Mr. Osbourne will call on you and give my news)

– I am Yours sincerely,

Robert Louis Stevenson

Address Apia, Samoa Copies of
Ballads, please, to Sidney
Colvin, British Museum

Letter to Henry James

Vailima, Apia, December 29th, 1890.

My dear Henry James, - It is terrible how little everybody writes, and how much of that little disappears in the capacious maw of the Post Office. Many letters, both from and to me, I now know to have been lost in transit: my eye is on the Sydney Post Office, a large ungainly structure with a tower, as being not a hundred miles from the scene of disappearance; but then I have no proof. THE TRAGIC MUSE you announced to me as coming; I had already ordered it from a Sydney bookseller: about two months ago he advised me that his copy was in the post; and I am still tragically museless...

Letter to Sidney Colvin

(On board ship between Sydney Apia, February 19 1891)

My dear Colvin, -

Have had a swingeing sharp attack in Sydney; beating the fields for two nights, Saturday and Sunday. Wednesday was brought on board, TEL QUEL, a wonderful wreck; and now, Wednesday week, am a good deal picked up, but yet not quite a Samson, being still groggy afoot and vague in the head. My chess, for instance, which is usually a pretty strong game, and defies all rivalry aboard, is vacillating, devoid of resource and observation, and hitherto not covered with customary laurels. As for work, it is impossible. We shall be in the saddle before long, no doubt, and the pen once more couched. You must not expect a letter under these circumstances, but be very thankful for a note. Once at Samoa, I shall try to resume my late excellent habits, and delight you with journals, you unaccustomed, I unaccustomed; but it is never too late to mend.

It is vastly annoying that I cannot go even to Sydney without an attack; and heaven knows my life was anodyne. I only once dined with anybody; at the (*Union*) club with (*Bernhard*) Wise; worked all morning - a terrible dead pull; a month only pro-duced the imperfect embryos of two chapters; lunched in the boarding-house, played on my pipe; went out and did some of my messages; dined at a French restaurant (*the Cosmopolitan Club*), and returned to play draughts, whist, or Van John with my family. This makes a cheery life after Samoa; but it isn't what you call burning the candle at both ends, is it? (It appears to me not one word of this letter will be legible by the time I am done with it, this dreadful ink rubs off.) I have a strange kind of novel under construction; it begins about 1660 and ends 1830, or perhaps I may continue it to 1875 or so, with another life. One, two, three, four, five, six generations, perhaps seven, figure therein; two of my old stories, 'Delafield' and 'Shovel,' are incorporated; it is to be told in the third person, with some of the brevity of history, some of the detail of romance. THE SHOVELS OF NEWTON FRENCH will be the name. The idea is an old one; it was brought to birth by an accident; a friend in the islands who picked up F. Jenkin, read a part, and said: 'Do you know, that's a strange book? I like it; I don't believe the public will; but I like it.'

He thought it was a novel! 'Very well,' said I, 'we'll see.'

It is but a little while since I lay sick in Sydney, beating the fields about the navy and Dean Swift and Dryden's Latin hymns; judge if I love this reinvigorating climate, where I can already toil till my head swims and every string in the poor jumping Jack (as he now lies in bed) aches with a kind of yearning strain, difficult to suffer in quiescence.

As for my damned literature, God knows what a business it is, grinding along without a scrap of inspiration or a note of style. But it has to be ground, and the mill grinds exceeding slowly though not particularly small. The last two chapters have taken me considerably over a month, and they

are still beneath pity. This I cannot continue, time not sufficing; and the next will just have to be worse. All the good I can express is just this; some day, when style revisits me, they will be excellent matter to rewrite...

Letter to Sidney Colvin

At sea, February 19 1893

My dear Colvin, - You will see from this heading that I am not dead yet nor likely to be. I was pretty considerably out of sorts, and that is indeed one reason why Fanny, Belle, and I have started out for a month's lark. To be quite exact, I think it will be about five weeks before we get home. We shall stay between two and three in Sydney. Already, though we only sailed yesterday, I am feeling as fit as a fiddle. Fanny ate a whole fowl for breakfast, to say nothing of a tower of hot cakes. Belle and I floored another hen betwixt the pair of us, and I shall be no sooner done with the present amanuensing racket than I shall put myself outside a pint of Guinness. If you think this looks like dying of consumption in Apia I can only say I differ from you. In the matter of *David* (*Balfour*), I have never yet received my proofs at all, but shall certainly wait for your suggestions. Certainly, Chaps. 17 to 20 are the hitch, and I confess I hurried over them with both wings spread. This is doubtless what you complain of. Indeed, I placed my single reliance on Miss Grant. If she couldn't ferry me over, I felt I had to stay there.

Three portraits of RLS by W. Barnett of Falk Studios, Sydney, 1893..

Letter to Sidney Colvin

At sea, April 1893

....I found my fame much grown on this return to civili-sation. DIGITO MONSTRARI is a new experience; people all looked at me in the streets in Sydney; and it was very queer. Here, of course, I am only the white chief in the Great House to the natives; and to the whites, either an ally or a foe. It is a much healthier state of matters. If I lived in an atmosphere of adulation, I should end by kicking against the pricks. O my beautiful forest, O my beautiful shining, windy house, what a joy it was to behold them again! No chance to take myself too seriously here. The difficulty of the end is the mass of matter to be attended to, and the small time left to transact it in. I mean from Alan's danger of arrest. But I have just seen my way out, I do believe.

Letter to Sidney Colvin

[*Vailima,   June   and   July   1891.*] MY DEAR COLVIN,—I am so hideously in arrears that I know not where to begin. However, here I am a prisoner in my room, unfit for work, incapable of reading with interest, and trying to catch up a bit. We have a guest here: a welcome guest: my Sydney music master, whose health broke down, and who came with his remarkable simplicity, to ask a month's lodging. He is newly married, his wife in the family way: beastly time to fall sick. I have found, by good luck, a job for him here which will pay some of his way: and in the meantime he is a pleasant guest, for he plays the flute with little sentiment but great perfection, and endears himself by his simplicity. To me, especially; I am so weary of finding people approach me with precaution, pick their words, flatter, and twitter; but the muttons of the good God are not at all afraid of the lion. They take him as he comes, and he does not bite—at least not hard. This makes us a party of 1, 2, 3, 4, 5, 6, 7, 8, at table; deftly waited on by Mary Carter, a very nice Sydney girl, who served us at a boarding-house and has since come on—how long she will endure this exile is another story; and gauchely waited on by Faauma, the new left-handed wife of the famed Lafaele, a little creature in native dress of course and as beautiful as a bronze candlestick, so fine, clean and dainty in every limb; her arms and her little hips in particular masterpieces. The rest of the crew may be stated briefly: the great Henry Simelé, still to the front; King, of the yellow beard, rather a disappointment—I am inclined on this point to republican opinions: Ratke, a German cook, good— and Germanly bad, he don't make *my* kitchen; Paul, now working out his debts outdoor; Emma, a strange weird creature—I suspect (from her colour) a quarter white— widow of a white man, ugly, capable, a really good laundress; Java—yes, that is the name—they spell it Siava, but pronounce it, and explain it Java—her assistant, a creature I adore from her plain, wholesome, bread-and-butter beauty…

Poem March 1893

These rings, O my beloved pair,
For me on your brown fingers wear:
Each, a perpetual caress,
To tell you of my tenderness.
Let - when at morning as ye rise
The golden topaz takes your eyes -
To each her emblem whisper sure
Love was awake an hour before.
Ah yes! an hour before ye woke
Low to my heart my emblem spoke,
And grave, as to renew an oath,

It I have kissed and blessed you both.
SYDNEY, N. S. W., March, 1893.

R. L. STEVENSON

Sydney News, 25 March 1893

Mr. Robert Louis Stevenson left by the Mariposa on Monday for his "Treasure Island." Although Mr Stevenson was only here for about three weeks, the effect of our climate began to make itself felt, and, much as he would like to have extended his trip, so as to visit Melbourne and Adelaide, it was evident that the sooner he returned the better it would be for his health. As usual, there was an immense crowd to see the American mail-boat off, and Mr. Stevenson had to divide the honor of being a distinguished traveller with Griffo and several other boxing celebrities. Mr. Stevenson, who remained on deck daring the entire time before the vessel swung into the stream, seemed to be acquainted with everyone, and was continually darting here and there over the deck, shaking hands with, first one and then another. Toe officers of the vessel, particularly, seemed pleased to have him back again, and he was universally greeted on board with a hearty welcome, while from the shore the many friends of the novelist waved him a farewell, coupled with best wishes for his future health and prosperity. The last seen of our visitor was from the stern of the boat, where he stood with his wife and mother-in-law, waving his hat cheerily to the people on the wharf.

Letter to Sidney Colvin

29   March   1893

'I was entertained at the General Assembly of the Pres-byterian Church; likewise at a sort of artistic club of a very rowdy character; made speeches at both and may therefore be said to have been like Saint Paul, all things to all men … Had some splendid photos taken, likewise a medallion by a French sculptor'.

On the eve of their arrival back in Samoa on 29 March 1893, he remarked to a friend that they had had 'some splendid photos taken … I am now very dandy; I announced two years ago that I should change. Slovenly youth, all right – not slovenly age. So really now I am pretty spruce: always a white shirt, white necktie, fresh shave, silk socks, O a great sight!'

Letter to Sidney Colvin

April 6 1893

…Fanny is not well, and we are miserably anxious'. I may as well say now that for . . . nearly eighteen months there has been something wrong; I could not write of it; but it was very trying and painful – and mostly fell on me. Now, we are face to face with the question: what next. The doctor has given her a medicine; we think it too strong, yet dare not stop it; and she passes from death-bed scenes to states of stupor. Ross, doctor in Sydney, warned me to expect trouble, so I'm not surprised; and happily Lloyd and Belle and I work together very smoothly, and none of us get excited.

'The doctor has come'… "There is no danger to life," he said twice. - "Is there any danger to mind?" I asked - "That is not excluded", said he'… "In Sydney…the first few weeks were delightful, her voice quiet again - no more of that anxious shrillness about nothing, that had so long echoed in my ears. And then she got bad again. Since she has been back, she has been kind - only querulously so, but

kind. And today's fit (which was the most insane she has yet had) was still only gentle and melancholy. I am broken on the wheel, or feel like it. Belle and Lloyd are both as good as gold. Belle has her faults and plenty of them; but she has been a blessed friend to me.

Letter to Henry James

Vailima Plantion, Samoan Islands, June 17th, 1893.

My dear Henry James, - I believe I have neglected a mail in answering yours. You will be very sorry to hear that my wife was exceedingly ill, and very glad to hear that she is better. I cannot say that I feel any more anxiety about her. We shall send you a photograph of her taken in Sydney in her customary island habit as she walks and gardens and shrilly drills her brown assistants. She was very ill when she sat for it, which may a little explain the appearance of the photograph. It reminds me of a friend of my grandmother's who used to say when talking to younger women, 'Aweel, when I was young, I wasnae just exactly what ye wad call BONNY, but I was pale, penetratin', and interestin'.' I would not venture to hint that Fanny is 'no bonny,' but there is no doubt but that in this pre-sentment she is 'pale, penetratin', and interesting.

As you are aware, I have been wading deep waters and con-tending with the great ones of the earth, not wholly without success. It is, you may be interested to hear, a dreary and infu-riating business. If you can get the fools to admit one thing, they will always save their face by denying another. If you can induce them to take a step to the right hand, they generally indemnify themselves by cutting a caper to the left. I always held (upon no evidence whatever, from a mere sentiment or intuition) that politics was the dirtiest, the most foolish, and the most random of human employments. I always held, but now I know it!

Fortunately, you have nothing to do with anything of the kind, and I may spare you the horror of further details….

Front cover by Percy Spence of the Sydney Illustrated News, March 25 1893.

STEVENSON IN
SYDNEY 1893

Rev. Will Burnett, from *I Can Remember Robert Louis Stevenson* (Chambers 1922)

STEVENSON came up to Sydney in February of 1893. It was not a very successful holiday, for he struck the season when the climate of Sydney is at its most depressing state. A combination of heat and moisture, suggestive of a Chinese laundry, a breeze from the ocean that brings no coolness but indeed an aggravation of discomfort, a night that is less refreshing than the day—these were not likely to make for Stevenson's health and comfort; and he spent part of the time in bed.

As might be expected it was through the Church that I came to meet him. I was then Minister of a Presbyterian Church in Sydney. It was the time of the General Assembly: and that clerical gathering, hearing that Stevenson was in the city, sent 'a deputation' (the proper course for a Church Court) to call on Stevenson in his hotel. The Assembly being not too numerous, the representative elders had the praise-worthy practice of providing lunch for the members everyday in the

Hotel Australia. The deputation, who (I think) found Stevenson sitting in his familiar position in bed with a writing-board on his knees, asked him to be the guest of the Assembly at one of these lunches, and he accepted the invitation. The joyful day arrived, the weather was slightly more agreeable, and the guest was able to be present.

I found myself not far from him, and able to study him when he rose to speak—a man rather over medium height, his height apparently increased by an exceeding thinness; a magician who drew to him your heart as well as your eyes. But it was your eyes first: they sought their joy in his. I don't think I have seen any portrait or photograph that conveys these eyes to me.

Some make them fat and far apart: others give them a 'sleekit' appearance. They may have had these evil qualities —I don't know,—the charm of them dispelled all critical faculty. He had not dressed for the part, nor had he dressed away from it (his taste for the bizarre was gone, and the accusation of studied indifference, not to say intended discourtesy, in dress is unsupported) ; he came as he liked to be, in what the tailor would describe as a lounge-suit, soft neck-wear, and a jacket of velvet. A duty hung upon that jacket, for the author's use of that jacket was characteristic.

He placed his two hands in the respective pockets, he took himself in charge, and gradually tightening his grip, appeared almost to reach breaking-point. He was very thin, and yet so full of life and energy! In the happiest vein himself, he spread happiness all round.

He cared no more for his appearance than we cared for it. I remember his saying somewhere that he never resented any (however inaccurate) description of himself save that of the American reporter who said: "Mr Stevenson had a tall willowy figure, surmounted by a classic head, from which issued a hacking cough.'

His speech was concerned, as may be imagined, with Scotland, Scotsmen, and the Scottish Church. One story ran somewhat like this. In his youth he was in bed suffering a childish sickness, and all the visitors to the house were visitors to his room. Among these visitors was a relative who had come to Edinburgh to attend the General Assembly. The Church was then rent over the organ question, and Master Stevenson was opposed to the views of Dr Robert Lee (of Old Greyfriars). When the relative was taking leave, little Louis raised a menacing finger, and thus warned him: 'You are going to the General Assembly. Whatever you do, have nothing to do with that man Lee.'

It is the atmosphere and magnetism of Robert Louis Stevenson's speech that remain in the memory, when the contents have long been absorbed. He spoke to those simple preachers with as much carefulness of style and virility of thought as if he had been addressing a gathering of literati. He spoke as if he enjoyed it, and would do anything to make his audience happy.

I felt then (and the feeling has been confirmed by every incident I read or hear of) that Stevenson possessed more than a genius for friendship; he had a good heart, whose goodness no evil fortune ever impaired. Perhaps that is the real source of such genius.

It was delightful in that place to hear a man speak with a good Scots accent. If he and I had met in the capital of Scotland we should have agreed that all Edinburgh men spoke the best of English without any accent at all. After a period of the cockney twang of New South Wales, I thought I detected symptoms of that drawl and turn which our enemies declare attend the man born in Edinburgh. It was none the less dear to me: the great author faded away: I heard the tones of a fellow-countryman, citizen with me of our own romantic town.

Through the friendship of the Rev. Dr Geikie, of Bathurst, a cousin of Sir Archibald and Professor James Geikie, I was allowed to join Stevenson and a few others after lunch in a private room of the Australia. I hope I took the modest part in the conversation that became a young man. I can remember that he spoke with keen interest of his family and its history, and, as events showed, he was at that very time collecting material for his Family of Engineers, which he was writing, and was finding the distance from Scotland a drawback. He was pleased to find a worshipper and constant student in that far-off city, and with the attentive charm of a royal personage he was interested to hear how intimately certain passages in my personal history were bound up with a paper-covered edition (the first by Arrowsmith of Bristol) of *Dr Jekyll and Mr Hyde*. We went our several ways. I saw him no more; but again I can remember how I got the news of his death, as it was passed almost from mouth to mouth in a Sydney suburban train. There was a distinct sense of personal loss, even in that pleasure-loving city, and among many who had never known him. It was not the way he thought to die: more tragic, more glorious perhaps. But nothing could lessen the grief of those who loved him, those who had basked even a short hour in the sunshine of his smile.

THE WRECKER

Every morning for the next two or three weeks, the stroke of ten found Norris, unkempt and haggard, at the lawyer's door. The long day and longer night he spent in the Domain, now on a bench, now on the grass under a Norfolk Island pine, the companion of perhaps the lowest class on earth, the Larrikins of Sydney. Morning after morning, the dawn behind the lighthouse recalled him from slumber; and he would stand and gaze upon the changing east, the fading lenses, the smokeless city, and the many-armed and many-masted harbour growing slowly clear under his eyes. His bed-fellows (so to call them) were less active; they lay sprawled upon the grass and benches, the dingy men, the frowsy women, prolonging their late repose; and Carthew wandered among the sleeping bodies alone, and cursed the incurable stupidity of his behaviour. Day brought a new society of nursery-maids and children, and fresh-dressed and (I am sorry to say) tight-laced maidens, and gay people in rich traps; upon the skirts of which Carthew and "the other blackguards"—his own bitter phrase--skulked, and chewed grass, and looked on. Day passed, the light died, the green and leafy precinct sparkled with lamps or lay in shadow, and the round of the night began again, the loitering women, the lurking men, the sudden outburst of screams, the sound of flying feet. "You mayn't believe it," says Carthew, "but I got to that pitch that I didn't care a hang. I have been wakened out of my sleep to hear a woman screaming, and I have only turned upon my other side. Yes, it's a queer place, where the dowagers and the kids walk all day, and at night you can hear people bawling for help as if it was the Forest of Bondy, with the lights of a great town all round, and parties spinning through in cabs from Government House and dinner with my lord!"

It was Norris's diversion, having none other, to scrape acquaintance, where, how, and with whom he could. Many a long dull talk he held upon the benches or the grass; many a strange waif he came to know; many strange things he heard, and saw some that were abominable. It was to one of these last that he owed his deliverance from the Domain. For some time the rain had been merciless; one night after another he had been obliged to squander fourpence on a bed and reduce his board to the remaining eightpence: and he sat one morning near the Macquarrie Street entrance, hungry, for he had gone without breakfast, and wet, as he had already been for several days, when the cries of an animal in distress attracted his attention. Some fifty yards away, in the extreme angle of the grass, a party of the chronically unemployed had got hold of a dog, whom they were torturing in a manner not to be described. The heart of Norris, which had grown indifferent to the cries of human anger or distress, woke at the appeal of the dumb creature. He ran amongst the Larrikins, scattered them, rescued the dog, and stood at bay. They were six in number, shambling gallows birds; but for once the proverb was right, cruelty was coupled with cowardice, and the wretches cursed him and made off. It chanced that this act of prowess had not passed unwitnessed. On a bench nearby there was seated a shopkeeper's assistant out of employ, a diminutive, cheerful, red-headed creature by the name of Hemstead. He was the last man to have interfered himself, for his discretion more than equalled his valour; but he made haste to congratulate Carthew, and to warn him he might not always be so fortunate.

"They're a dyngerous lot of people about this park. My word! it doesn't do to ply with them!" he observed, in that RYCY AUSTRYLIAN English, which (as it has received the imprimatur of Mr. Froude) we should all make haste to imitate.

"Why, I'm one of that lot myself," returned Carthew. Hemstead laughed and remarked that he knew a gentleman when he saw one.

"For all that, I am simply one of the unemployed," said Carthew, seating himself beside his new acquaintance, as he had sat (since this experience began) beside so many dozen others.

"I'm out of a plyce myself," said Hemstead.

"You beat me all the way and back," says Carthew. "My trouble is that I have never been in one."

"I suppose you've no tryde?" asked Hemstead.

"I know how to spend money," replied Carthew, "and I really do know something of horses and something of the sea. But the unions head me off; if it weren't for them, I might have had a dozen berths."

"My word!" cried the sympathetic listener. "Ever try the mounted police?" he inquired.

"I did, and was bowled out," was the reply; "couldn't pass the doctors."

"Well, what do you think of the ryleways, then?"

asked Hemstead.

"What do YOU think of them, if you come to that?" asked Carthew.

"O, - I - don't think of them; I don't go in for manual labour," said the little man proudly. "But if a man don't mind that, he's pretty sure of a job there."

"By George, you tell me where to go!" cried Carthew, rising. The heavy rains continued, the country was already overrun with floods; the railway system daily required more hands, daily the superintendent advertised; but "the unemployed" preferred the resources of charity and rapine, and a navvy, even an amateur navvy, commanded money in the market. The same night, after a tedious journey, and a change of trains to pass a landslip, Norris found himself in a muddy cutting behind South Clifton, attacking his first shift of manual labour. For weeks the rain scarce relented. The whole front of the mountain slipped seaward from above, avalanches of clay, rock, and uprooted forest spewed over the cliffs and fell upon the beach or in the breakers. Houses were carried bodily away and smashed like nuts; others were menaced and deserted, the door locked, the chimney cold, the dwellers fled elsewhere for safety. Night and day the fire blazed in the encampment; night and day hot coffee was served to the over-driven toilers in the shift; night and day the engineer of the section made his rounds with words of encouragement, hearty and rough and well suited to his men. Night and day, too, the telegraph clicked with disastrous news and anxious inquiry. Along the terraced line of rail, rare trains came creeping and signalling; and paused at the threatened corner, like living things con-scious of peril. The commandant of the post would hastily review his labours, make (with a dry throat) the signal to advance; and the whole squad line the way and look on in a choking silence, or burst into a brief cheer as the train cleared the point of danger and shot on, perhaps through the thin sunshine between squalls, perhaps with blinking lamps into the gathering, rainy twilight.

One such scene Carthew will remember till he dies. It blew great guns from the seaward; a huge surf bombarded, five hundred feet below him, the steep mountain's foot; close in was a vessel in distress, firing shots from a fowling-piece, if any help might come. So he saw and heard her the moment before the train appeared and paused, throwing up a Babylonian tower of smoke into the rain, and oppressing men's hearts with the scream of her whistle. The engineer was there himself; he paled as he made the signal: the engine came at a foot's pace; but the whole bulk of mountain shook and seemed to nod seaward, and the watching navvies instinctively clutched at shrubs and trees: vain precautions, vain as the shots from the poor sailors. Once again fear was disappointed; the train passed unscathed; and Norris, drawing a long breath, remembered the labouring ship and glanced below. She was gone.

So the days and the nights passed: Homeric labour in Homeric circumstance. Carthew was sick with sleeplessness and coffee; his hands, softened by the wet, were cut to ribbons; yet he enjoyed a peace of mind and health of body hitherto unknown. Plenty of open air, plenty of physical exertion, a continual instancy of toil; here was what had been hitherto lacking in that misdirected life, and the true cure of vital scepticism. To get the train through: there was the recurrent problem; no time remained to ask if it were necessary. Carthew, the idler, the spendthrift, the drifting dilettant, was soon remarked, praised, and advanced. The engineer swore by him and pointed him out for an example.

"I've a new chum, up here," Norris overheard him saying,

"a young swell. He's worth any two in the squad." The words fell on the ears of the discarded son like music; and from that moment, he not only found an interest, he took a pride, in his plebeian tasks.

The press of work was still at its highest when quarter-day approached. Norris was now raised to a position of some trust; at his discretion, trains were stopped or forwarded at the dangerous cornice near North Clifton; and he found in this responsibility both terror and delight. The thought of the seventy-five pounds that would soon await him at the lawyer's, and of his own obligation to be present every quarter-day in Sydney, filled him for a little with divided councils. Then he made up his mind, walked in a slack moment to the inn at Clifton, ordered a sheet of paper and a bottle of beer, and wrote, explaining that he held a good appointment which he would lose if he came to Sydney, and asking the lawyer to accept this letter as an evidence of his presence in the colony, and retain the money till next quarter-day. The answer came in course of post, and was not merely favourable but cordial. "Although what you propose is contrary to the terms of my instructions," it ran, "I willingly accept the responsibility of granting your request. I should say I am agreeably disappointed in your behaviour. My experience has not led me to found much expectations on gentlemen in your position."

The rains abated, and the temporary labour was discharged; not Norris, to whom the engineer clung as to found money; not Norris, who found himself a ganger on the line in the regular staff of navvies. His camp was pitched in a grey wilderness of rock and forest, far from any house; as he sat with his mates about the evening fire, the trains passing on the track were their next and indeed their only neighbours, except the wild things of the wood. Lovely weather, light and monotonous employment, long hours of somnolent camp-fire talk, long sleepless nights, when he reviewed his foolish and fruitless career as he rose and walked in the moonlit forest, an occasional paper of which he would read all, the advertisements with as much relish as the text: such was the tenor of an existence which soon began to weary and harass him. He lacked and regretted the fatigue, the furious hurry, the suspense, the fires, the midnight coffee, the rude and mud-bespattered poetry of the first toilful weeks. In the quietness of his new surroundings, a voice summoned him from this exorbital part of life, and about the middle of October he threw up his situation and bade farewell to the camp of tents and the shoulder of Bald Mountain.

Clad in his rough clothes, with a bundle on his shoulder and his accumulated wages in his pocket, he entered Sydney for the second time, and walked with pleasure and some bewilderment in the cheerful streets, like a man landed from a voyage. The sight of the people led him on. He forgot his necessary errands, he forgot to eat. He wandered in moving multitudes like a stick upon a river. Last he came to the Domain and strolled there, and remembered his shame and sufferings, and looked with poignant curiosity at his successors. Hemstead, not much shabbier and no less cheerful than before, he recognised and addressed like an old family friend.

"That was a good turn you did me," said he. "That railway was the making of me. I hope you've had luck yourself."

"My word, no!" replied the little man. "I just sit here and read the Dead Bird. It's the depression in tryde, you see. There's no positions goin' that a man like me would care to look at." And he showed Norris his certificates and written characters, one from a grocer in Wooloomooloo, one from an ironmonger, and a third from a billiard saloon. "Yes," he said, "I tried bein' a billiard marker. It's no account; these lyte hours are no use for a man's health. I won't be no man's slyve," he added firmly.

On the principle that he who is too proud to be a slave is usually not too modest to become a pensioner, Carthew gave him half a sovereign, and departed, being suddenly struck with hunger, in the direction of the Paris House. When he came to that quarter of the city, the barristers were trotting in the streets in wig and gown, and he stood to observe them with his bundle on his shoulder, and his mind full of curious recollections of the past.

"By George!" cried a voice, "it's Mr. Carthew!"

And turning about he found himself face to face with a handsome sunburnt youth, somewhat fatted, arrayed in the finest of fine raiment, and sporting about a sovereign's worth of flowers in his buttonhole. Norris had met him during his first days in Sydney at a farewell supper; had even escorted him on board a schooner full of cockroaches and black-boy sailors, in which he was bound for six months among the islands; and had kept him ever since in entertained remembrance. Tom Hadden (known to the bulk of Sydney folk as Tommy) was heir to a considerable property, which a prophetic father had placed in the hands of rigorous trustees. The income supported Mr. Hadden in splendour for about three months out of twelve; the rest of the year he passed in retreat among the islands. He was now about a week returned from his eclipse, pervading Sydney in hansom cabs and airing the first bloom of six new suits of clothes; and yet the unaffected creature hailed Carthew in his working jeans and with the damning bundle on his shoulder, as he might have claimed acquaintance with a duke.

"Come and have a drink!" was his cheerful cry.

"I'm just going to have lunch at the Paris House," returned

Carthew. "It's a long time since I have had a decent meal."

"Splendid scheme!" said Hadden. "I've only had breakfast half an hour ago; but we'll have a private room, and I'll manage to pick something. It'll brace me up. I was on an awful tear last night, and I've met no end of fellows this morning." To meet a fellow, and to stand and share a drink, were with Tom synonymous terms.

They were soon at table in the corner room up-stairs, and paying due attention to the best fare in Sydney. The odd similarity of their positions drew them together, and they began soon to exchange confidences. Carthew related his privations in the Domain and his toils as a navvy; Hadden gave his experience as an amateur copra merchant in the South Seas, and drew a humorous picture of life in a coral island.

Of the two plans of retirement, Carthew gathered that his own had been vastly the more lucrative; but Hadden's trading outfit had consisted largely of bottled stout and brown sherry for his own consumption.

"I had champagne too," said Hadden, "but I kept that in case of sickness, until I didn't seem to be going to be sick, and then I opened a pint every Sunday. Used to sleep all morning, then breakfast with my pint of fizz, and lie in a hammock and read Hallam's *Middle Ages*. Have you read that? I always take something solid to the islands. There's no doubt I did the thing in rather a fine style; but if it was gone about a little cheaper, or there were two of us to bear the expense, it ought to pay hand over fist. I've got the influence, you see. I'm a chief now, and sit in the speak-house under my own strip of roof. I'd like to see them taboo ME! They daren't try it; I've a strong party, I can tell you. Why, I've had upwards of thirty cowtops sitting in my front verandah eating tins of salmon."

"Cowtops?" asked Carthew, "what are they?"

"That's what Hallam would call feudal retainers," explained Hadden, not without vainglory. "They're My Followers. They belong to My Family. I tell you, they come expensive, though; you can't fill up all these retainers on tinned salmon for nothing; but whenever I could get it, I would give 'em squid. Squid's good for natives, but I don't care for it, do you?--or shark either. It's like the working classes at home. With copra at the price it is, they ought to be willing to bear their share of the loss; and so I've told them again and again. I think it's a man's duty to open their minds, and I try to, but you can't get political economy into them; it doesn't seem to reach their intelligence."

The Writer's Walk plaque at Circular Quay, Sydney.

Portrait of RLS by Gerilamo Nerli, 1892.

TIMELINE

1890

January

10: RLS signs the deed for the purchase of Vailima Estate, Apia, Samoa.

February

4: Leaves Apia on the Lübeck.

13: Arrives in Sydney, staying at the Union Club, Bent Street, working on *The Wrecker*.

14: Argus published *RLS: His Views on Samoan Affairs. Newcastle Morning Herald* published *A Well Known Novelist in Sydney*.

22: *Launceston Examiner* published *RLS: A Novelist's Tour in the Pacific*.

22: *The Treasure of Franchard* serialised in the *Goulburn Evening Penny Post*.

Visits Charles Kerry's photographic studio at 308 George Street.

25: RLS writes his *Father Damien* letter at the Union Club.

March

24: The Damien Letter published in *The Australian Star*. 27:
Copies of the limited edition *Father Damien: An Open Letter to
the Reverend Dr. Hyde of Honolulu* posted from Sydney by RLS,
most with annotations.

April-July

11: Leaves Sydney on the Janet Nicoll, cruising
Auckland, New Zealand, the Tokelau Islands,
Cooks Islands, Ellice Islands, Gilbert Islands, Marshall
Islands, New Caledonia, New Hebrideans and
Noumea, amongst other places The cruise fin-ishes on
26 July 1890 in Noumea, New Caledonia.

May

10: Publication of *Father Damien: An Open Letter to Reverend
Doctor Hyde* in *Elele*.

24: *Australian Star* published *Robert Louis Stevenson*.

July

27: Fanny and Lloyd depart for Sydney, RLS stays in Noumea.

August

7: RLS arrives in Sydney, staying at the Union Club, working
on *The Wrecker* [1892], *The Ebb-Tide* [1894], *Island Nights' Entertainments* [1893], *The South Seas* (1896) and *Ballads* [1890).

18: RLS sends 15 chapters of *The South Seas* to London
with Lloyd Osborne.

September

5: Leaves Sydney for Apia with Fanny on the Lübeck.

December

13: Publication of RLS poems *Ballads* in London.

1891

January

6: Leaves Apia for Sydney on the Lübeck
16: RLS's mother, Margaret Stevenson, with Lloyd Osborne, arrived in Melbourne on the *Lusitania*.

20: RLS arrives in Sydney, and all stay at the Oxford Hotel.

26: RLS and his mother move to Mrs Leaney's boarding house, 17 St Mary's Terrace, Wooloomooloo.

Henry Walter Barnett photographs RLS.

February

RLS dines with Bernhard Wise at the Union Club, Cosmopolitan Club, the Australian and Atheneum Clubs.

6: *The South Seas* begins serialization in *Black and White*, RLS writing new sections on 'Imperial Australian Vellum'.

7: RLS interview with the *Australian Star*.

8: RLS ill, stays in bed at the Union Club.

14: *The South Seas* begins serialization in the *Daily Telegraph* (Sydney).

14: Portrait of RLS from a photograph by Charles Kerry published in the *Australian Town & Country Journal*.
18: Leaves Sydney with his mother on the Lübeck.

March

1: Returns to Samoa with mother.

13: *Illustrated Sydney News* publishes portrait of RLS in Sydney.

April

2-13: Sails around the Samoan islands in Nukunona.

May

16: Margaret Stevenson moves into Vailima.

31: *Freemans Journal* published RLS Defence letter.

August

Serialization of *The Wrecker* (with Lloyd) begins in *Scribner's* to July 1892.

September

The Daily Telegraph (Sydney), serializes *In the South Seas*.

November

7: Finishes writing *The Wrecker* (with Lloyd Osborne).

10: *Sydney Morning Herald* publishes *RLS: Early Homes and Haunts*.

December

12: *Australian Town & Country Journal* publish column titled *RLS*.

1892

An Object of Pity; or, the Man Haggard, A Romance. By Many Competant Hands published in Sydney.

January

9: *Life Under the Equator* serialised in the *Clarence & Richmond Examiner*.

February

13: Begins writing *Catriona* (1893).

April

6: Publication of *Across the Plains*.

June

25: Publication of *The Wrecker*.

August

Girolamo Nerli arrives in Samoa for a two month visit and painted a portrait of RLS.

6: Graham Balfour arrives at Vailima and stays with RLS.

8: Publication of *A Footnote to History*.

September

26: Finishes *Catriona*.

December

7: *The Pot of Gold* and *Uma or the Beach of Falesa*, serialized in the *Australian Town and Country Journal*.

1893

January

11: Margaret Stevenson arrives in Sydney, staying at the Oxford Hotel. After a short stay she goes to Melbourne to visit her sister.

February

18: Leaves Apia on the S.S. *Mariposa* with Fanny and Belle.

24: Arrives in Auckland, RLS visits Sir George Gray at the Northern Club.

28: Arrives in Sydney, stays at the Oxford Hotel, Sydney.

March

1: SMH published *RLS: His Samoan Experiences.*

2: Margaret Stevenson arrives in Sydney from Melbourne.

Photographed by Charles Kerry, in a family group photograph by Freeman, and 8 portraits by Henry William Barnett of Falk & Co.

7: Guest of the 28th General Assembly of the Presbyterian Church.

Sculpted by Leyselle, a medallion which has not survived.

Working on the final version of *The Ebb Tide.*

10: Speech at the Thistle Club, Sydney.

Taken to the Artist's camp at Edwards Beach, by JF Archibald and Julian Ashton, meeting Arthur Streeton, Tom Roberts, Percy Spence, and old friend Arthur Daplyn.

Speech at the Australia Hotel, mid-March.

13: Margaret Stevenson read his *Missions in the South Seas* to the Women's Missionary Association, in Quong Tart's Rooms, Sydney.

14: Luncheon with the Presbyterian Assembly.

Staying with Andrew Garran, at Strathmore, 229 Bridge Road, Forest Lodge.

15: *Sydney Morning Herald* published *Mr R.L. Stevenson and the Presbyterian Church.*

Daily Telegraph reports on this as an *An After-Luncheon Speech by RLS.*

16: Lecture on France at the Cosmopolitan Club, Wynyard Square, with Bernhard Wise.

Visit to the Royal Exchange and to Sydney University.

17: *Sydney Morning Herald* published RLS speech at the Cosmo-politan Club. Also sat for a pencil portrait by Percy Spence.

18: *Mr. R. L. Stevenson and the Assembly* published in *The Presbyterian*, along with his *Missions in the South Seas.*

Sydney Doctor Fairfax Ross told RLS that he was suffering from "exposure, malaria, worry and over-work", and was also consulted about Fanny Stevenson's mental health.

20:Leaves Sydney on the *Mariposa*.

25: *The Presbyterian* publishes *The Labour Traffic*.

25: Cover of *Illustrated Sydney News* shows a Percy Spence cartoon of RLS.

28: *Riverina Grazier* published RLS interview as *The Labour Traffic.*

30: Returns to Vailima, working on *Weir of Hermiston* (1896) and *The Ebb-Tide* (1894).

April

6: Publication of *Island Nights' Entertainments.*

May

5: *Westminister Budget* publishes *Mr. Robert Louis Stevenson at Work and Play* by Tighe Ryan.

June

18: Sends last two chapters of *The Ebb-Tide* to Sidney Colvin.

David Balfour serialised in the *Australian Town and Country Journal.*

July

14: *The Story of a Dog* by Mrs Stevenson is published in the

The Stevenson's piano from Vailima, now at the MAAS, Sydney. Below: A sketch of RLS by Blaski.

Albury Banner & Wodonga Express.

September

2: Serialisation of *Kidnapped* begins in the *Northern Star* (Lismore).

12: Travels to Honolulu on SS *Mariposa*.

18: *Sydney Morning Herald* publishes *RLS Dreams: A Remarkable Letter.*

October

27: Leaves Hawaii for Samoa.

November

Returns to Samoa.

Alfred James Daplyn arrived in Samoa from Sydney to paint a portrait of RLS, and shared a memoir of their times together in France.

1894

March

24: *The Ebb Tide* serialised in the *Northern Star* (Lismore).

May

5: *Robert Louis Stevenson: A Visit to His Home in Samoa* by Arthur Daplyn published in the *Daily Telegraph* (Sydney).

18: Margaret Stevenson and Graham Balfour arrive in Sydney *en-route* to Samoa, leaving for New Zealand on June 11.

August

Publication of "My First Book: Treasure Island" in *The Idler*

September

21: Publication of *The Ebb-Tide* (with Lloyd Osbourne).

November

13: Feast celebrating RLS's 44th birthday.

December

3: Dies of a cerebral hemorrhage

4: Buried on the summit of Mount Vaea on Upolu, Samoa.

NOTES

1. *Vide Sydney Morning Herald*, September 23 1933:
'Stevenson and the Union Club'

2. *Vide Sydney Morning Herald*, December 28 1933

3. Mr. Sanders is not correct in his details. Search reveals that the Damien Article was printed on the middle page of the *Star* on May 24. Miss Ida Leeson, the Mitchell Librarian, has the following note concerning the publication of the various editions:-''Mr. White (*Sydney Morning Herald*, January 2, 1934) is evidently correct that the *Star* was not the first publication. J. M. Sanders, managing editor of the *Star* at the time it published the letter, stated with much circumstantial detail that it was. But reference to the *Star* of May 24, 1890, and the matter accompanying Stevenson 's letter, disproves so much of his recollection that the rest cannot be accepted. Stevenson had left Sydney six weeks (the *Star*'s own statement) when the *Star* published. The *Scot's Observer*, according to all bibliographical records, published on May 3 and 10, 1890. The only proof we can find for March 27, 1890, as the date of [the Sydney] pamphlet publication is the bibliography in Balfour's

Life of Stevenson. J. M. Sanders gives details to show that it was printed after the appearance in the *Star*. But, if this were so, it might easily have been later than the first published edition by Chatto and Windus, reprinted from the *Scot's Observer*." The date given by Stevenson at the beginning of the letter is February 25, 1890; the edition of the *Elele* in which it appeared at Honolulu is dated May 10, 1890.

4. This, of course, is incorrect; there was no imprint.-G. M.

5. See *A Bibliography of the Complete Works of R. L. Stevenson*, by J. Herbert Slater, London (Bell, 1914), p. 45.

6. Now demolished. It was exactly opposite St. James' Church, near Phillip Street.

7. *Vide* J. Tighe Ryan's article in *The Catholic Record*, Vol.V111.

8. This is reproduced in *Stevensonia*, opp. p. 329.

9. *Vide The Presbyterian*, March 18, 1893, where the address is reported in full.

10. Tragic because his wife had been ill all the time, and living on a diet of maltine and slops.-G. M.

www.ingramcontent.com/pod-product-compliance
Lightning Source LLC
Chambersburg PA
CBHW030959090426
42737CB00007B/605